M000214641

"Every exceptional child needs an exceptional mother. *Remembering Terri* is the story of Terri and her mother Janice. Janice takes the reader on an emotional journey of the challenge of raising an exceptional child – the disappointments, triumphs, joys, and heartbreak. And the devastating, heart wrenching loss of Terri. Janice's description of her grief and raw emotions are not easy to read, and I know weren't easy to share. Their story will touch your heart.

Terri was my student and friend. We were together for many years. Terri was generous with her love – a love that is cherished by all who were fortunate to know her."

— FAITH BROOME

"Sarah Palin once said, 'Children with special needs inspire a very special love.' *Remembering Terri* is an up close and honest look at the blessings as well as the challenges, the fears, and the frustrations of parenting a child with special needs and the special love shared by this mom and her daughter. It is also the story of a brokenhearted mom and her efforts to find peace after her daughter's sudden and unexpected death.

Those who knew Terri will enjoy the way Remembering Terri so marvelously captures the essence of Terri – her fun loving ways, her laughter, and her loving spirit. Those who parent children with special needs and those parents grieving the death of child will find inspiration and encouragement in this book.

I had the joy of knowing Terri and the privilege of serving as her pastor. She made us a better church."

— TIM ANDERSON

❧

REMEMBERING

Terri

a memoir of
extraordinary love,
unimaginable sadness,
and remarkable courage

JANICE CAMERON STEELE

I dedicate this book to my daughter,
Terri Renee Ledbetter.
I love you forever.

CONTENTS

THE SPECIAL CHILD

The child, yet unborn, spoke with the Father
"Lord, how will I survive in the world?
I will not be like other children. My
walk may be slower, my speech hard
to understand, I may look different.
What is to become of me?"
The Lord replied to the child,
"My precious one, have no fear, I will
give you exceptional parents. They
will love you because you are special,
not in spite of it. Though your path
through life will be difficult, your
reward will be greater, you have been
blessed with a special ability to love,
and those who lives you touch will
be blessed because you are special.

— UNKNOWN AUTHOR

FOREWORD

These pages tell the story of my special needs child – her struggles, her triumphs, and her death. Her full name is Terri Renee Ledbetter.

She was a loving, caring, compassionate person, a beautiful girl inside and out. She was brave with a beautiful laugh. She never met a stranger and loved people unconditionally. Everyone she met instantly fell in love with her. Her laughter was infectious.

To see her smiling face brought joy to my heart. My friend, Terry said, "She left a handprint on every heart she ever touched."

She was developmentally delayed since birth as the result of anoxia (an insufficient amount of oxygen to the brain). She was a child in an adult's body. If this wasn't enough, she was diagnosed with schizophrenia at age 19. She suffered from extreme anxiety and debilitating migraine headaches. Only other parents of special needs children can understand the intense emotions of raising a child with special needs. I take great pride in knowing I helped my daughter live her life to the fullest.

Terri didn't want to be special or sick. She wanted to be like everyone else. She wanted to drive a car, get married, and have a family. Knowing she would never do these things brought me great heartache.

We loved each other with an incredible love. We were inseparable. As many parents feel about their children, our bond was strong. I thank God he chose me to be her mother. What a blessing!

PART I

TERRI'S STORY

Terri, age 2, 1974

1

TRAUMATIC BIRTH

December 16, 1971 – *Little did I know I would hear my daughter, Terri, repeat this date over and over again throughout her life.*

I was at work when suddenly I felt a sharp pain in my stomach. The pain was so severe; I sensed something was terribly wrong. Eight months pregnant with my first baby, I called my husband.

"Maybe it's something you ate for lunch," he said.

"Please come," I moaned.

My sister, Diane, worked close by so he called to ask her to check on me. When she arrived, I was vomiting and hemorrhaging. She called my doctor. "Don't wait on an ambulance, put her in the back seat of a car and bring her immediately to the emergency room," he said.

By the time my husband had arrived my pants and shoes were soaked in blood. Embarrassed to walk out in front of the men working there, I asked him to carry me. As we went to get in the car, another car had blocked us in. Every second was crucial for me and my baby. The men at the Auto Parts House rushed to push the car out of our way and we sped to the hospital. The hospital was thirty minutes away.

My doctor was waiting when I arrived and immediately diagnosed a placental abruption–when the placenta separates from the uterus prior to birth. According to the American Pregnancy Association if the abruption is severe, 15% of the babies die. For those who survive, 40-50% have a chance of developing long-term health complications due to the lack of oxygen in the uterus and premature birth. (https://www.birthinjuryguide.org/birth-injury/causes/placental-abruption/, assessed June 13, 2019)

Since my condition was critical and required immediate surgery, my doctor needed another surgeon to assist him. As sick as I was, I remember him going to the window and calling out across the parking lot for another doctor. Suddenly I was wheeling down the corridor to the operating room. Later, confused from the anesthesia after a cesarean section, I asked the nurse, "Has my baby been born yet?"

"You didn't hear her cry?" she asked.

My first thought, *it's a girl and she is alive*. My doctor told me it was a miracle my baby survived, "one in a million," he said.

She weighed in at four pounds and 11 ounces. We named her Terri Renee Ledbetter. In 1971, premature babies were not allowed outside of the nursery. It was the next day before I was strong enough to walk around to the nursery to see her for the first time. As every mother knows, I was in awe of her. She was beautiful and perfect in every way.

I was staring through the glass window at the incubator that held her, with tears streaming down my face, when my twin sister appeared and threw her arms around me. I was stunned to see her. Back then the only people allowed on the maternity floor were the daddies and grandparents. Our visit only lasted a couple of minutes before the security guard came and promptly escorted her off the floor. "Didn't you hear me? You are not allowed on this floor."

Joyce was crying, "You don't understand. I drove all the way from Mississippi to see my twin sister and her baby."

I was crying harder than before. "Joyce, go with the security guard. I will be home in a few days." The security guard had to literally drag her off the floor.

That same day her husband, Wayne, came bouncing in my hospital room. I was glad to see him, yet baffled. "How did you get in here? The security guard dragged Joyce off the floor screaming and crying earlier today."

"I told the receptionist I was the daddy! She didn't question me, so here I am," he said.

I was worried one of the nurses would notice Wayne was not my husband. That didn't happen. We had a nice long visit and he reported back to my twin sister that I was okay and so was the baby.

I was released to go home after seven days. It would be another two weeks and four days before Terri gained up to five and one-half pounds, the required weight for preemies to be released from the hospital. I was thirty minutes away from her with no way to get there. I had just had surgery and couldn't drive. My husband was a full-time college student and worked a second shift job, so he wasn't in a position to take me to the hospital for visits. I called every day and went as often as I found a way. It was the longest two weeks and four days of my life. The long anticipated day finally arrived and I brought my baby home. I dressed her in the cutest pink outfit, bonnet included. My mother-in-law held and cuddled her as I drove the 30 miles home.

I already loved her with all of my heart and soul. I was totally devoted to her and wanted to be the perfect mom. We purchased a small portable crib. At night I placed the crib next to my bed and rested my hand on her back as she slept. I needed to know she was breathing. In 1971, it was the custom to place babies on their stomach to sleep.

She had only been home a few days when she developed colic. By the way, home was a single-wide mobile home next door to my parent's home. Her pediatrician changed her formula, yet the colic persisted for what seemed like weeks on end. She would scream and scream. There was no pacifying her. Thank God for my Momma. With her help and the help of Terri's paternal grandmother, we survived those awful months and settled into a close and loving mother and daughter relationship.

After a couple of months at home, I needed to return to work, so we hired Reola to take care of Terri. She cooked and cleaned, but most importantly she took exceptional care of Terri. I enjoyed coming in from a long day to a clean house and warm meal. It freed me up to spend my time with Terri.

Reola came to work every day in a white uniform and hair net. She didn't drive so her husband brought her. She was dependable; I don't think she missed a single day in the three years she cared for Terri. We were blessed to have her. She loved Terri and Terri loved her.

My daughter was a beautiful child–blond hair and blue eyes. Everywhere we went people would comment on how pretty she was. Her granddaddy, Roy, said she had "Miss America" legs. I can see her bouncing around the house in her walker making those adorable baby sounds. Most of the time she was a happy child; I was the epitome of a proud parent. Life was good.

Terri, 1976

2

EARLY DEVELOPMENT

For the first few years Terri's development appeared to be normal for the most part. She took her first step on her first birthday (not bad for a preemie). She was so excited at her party. I still remember the blue dress she wore. She loved her birthday cake; she was covered in icing from head to toe.

She was a little slow at toilet training. It didn't set off any real alarm for her pediatrician, yet it concerned me because I remembered her traumatic birth. I compared her to Joyce's son, Cameron. He was only eight months younger than Terri, yet appeared to be developing at a faster pace. His room was organized; every toy had its place. When Terri came to play, she destroyed it in no time, toys thrown everywhere. And of course, she couldn't remember how to put them back in their places. He never minded picking up after her. They enjoyed playing together.

Terri experienced a traumatic childhood accident. She was two years old when she and her cousin, Elizabeth, were swinging on the swing set in the back yard. A commotion next door had caught the attention of me and my twin sister for a moment. When we turned back around, Terri was lying on the ground. I rushed to pick her up. She was unconscious. Since the commotion next door involved a police officer, I yelled for him to come to our rescue. He called an ambulance; we waited and waited for it to come. After a few minutes, she came around and threw up. Her pediatrician met us at the hospital. He admitted her for overnight observation for a possible concussion, but she was eating and playing in no time and released to come home the next day. I was thankful God had kept her safe.

Terri was admitted to the hospital one other time when she was three years old. My husband picked her up at childcare like he usually did. She was asleep. When the worker went to wake her, she was practically nonresponsive. He rushed her to the emergency room. By the time they arrived at the hospital she was convulsing. When her pediatrician examined her, her temperature was 104. He did a spinal tap to rule out meningitis. The test came back negative. She recovered quickly and was released the next day with only an antibiotic for a sore throat. Once again I thanked God my baby was okay.

Terri's illness gave everyone a huge scare at her daycare center, because a young girl had passed away a few weeks earlier with Reye's syndrome. Afterward the workers were vigilant with all the children; they called me if Terri had a temperature of 100.

Joyce decided she wanted to surprise Momma and Daddy at Christmas with a group photograph of their four grandchildren. Chris was eight years old, Elizabeth was five, Terri was three, and Cameron was the baby at age two. I dressed her in a red dress with matching hair bow. She was adorable.

All of the grandchildren posed and were perfect little angels with the exception of Terri. She could not sit still and screamed nonstop. I was perplexed and couldn't understand why she would cry for no apparent reason. We finally had to call it a day without a picture. My sister tried to comfort me by telling me not to be upset. I couldn't be consoled and she couldn't conceal her disappointment. Why wasn't Terri like her cousins? It was a hard day.

At age four Terri wasn't talking, at least not in sentences. She could say a few words such as momma, daddy, book, or tea. Yes, back then we didn't know better, we let her sip from our tea glass. There were no sippy cups in those days! She pointed and cried when she wanted something and stood in front of the refrigerator when she was hungry. One time when we came home from a visit at her grandparent's, she wouldn't stop crying. I tried everything I could think of. Finally, I realized she wanted her stuffed doggie, Charlie. He had been left in the back seat of our car. I quickly retrieved him and soon she was sound asleep. How much easier our lives would have been if Terri could only talk.

Since Terri's speech was noticeably delayed, her pediatrician suggested we take her to Hall Institute in Columbia, South Carolina, for evaluation. An appointment was made and my husband and I anticipated the trip to Columbia with great concern. Alicia, a psychologist, administered a battery of developmental tests. "Hello Terri, my name is Alicia. Let's go and play some games. We'll have lots of fun together." Terri liked the idea of games, so she was happy to go. After testing we went to the lab for a blood draw to rule out any genetic abnormalities. In Alicia's analysis she told us to expect our daughter to be a "little slow" in her development, probably a result of the anoxia suffered at birth. Speech therapy was recommended. My husband and I were devastated. I cried for weeks.

Trying to process this heartbreaking prognosis, we rationalized: maybe our child could benefit from being around other children. We placed Terri in a local childcare. The owner had a special needs child and was more than willing to accept her. She received excellent care. One of the workers was devoted to her and gave Terri her undivided attention. Much to our dismay, we did not notice any great strides in her development–our fears heightened.

My daughter and I began the weekly trips out of town for speech therapy. She shared her sessions with male twins. Their mother and I watched through a one-way glass. Terri was excited to participate and gave it her best, while the twins were quiet and withdrawn. I was thrilled with her eagerness to learn though the progress was slow. We continued therapy until she entered kindergarten. Once she reached school age, the school system provided her with speech therapy.

We desperately wanted her to be like other children and communicate with us better. So much so my mother-in-law suggested we take her to a spiritual healer. It was months down the road before he would be in our area. The time finally came and on a Sunday afternoon, her grandmother and I drove her to Greenville where we stood in line with hundreds of people. Terri was impatient, so I took her outside to play while her grandmother held our place in line with a glimmer of hope she would be healed. As I came back inside the church, the spiritual healer was leaving and walked past us. I grabbed him by the coat tail, "My daughter's speech is delayed. Will you please help us?" He touched her forehead, said a few words I did not recognize and was gone. We didn't notice any change in her speech; yet, much later when she finally began to talk in sentences, it was a language explosion. She never quit talking, repeating the same things over and over again.

3

DIVORCE

W hen Terri was four years old, her father and I divorced. My father remodeled one of his rental houses and allowed us to live there rent free. It was a cozy four-room house and perfect for the two of us. I was more concerned for Terri than I was for myself. She would stand at the picture glass window in the den and cry for her daddy for hours at a time.

There was a song popular at the time, *Me and You Against the World,* by Helen Reddy. This song described my feelings. I felt like we were all alone in the world. We were struggling to get by. In her childlike way Terri knew she could count on me to be there for her. And we knew God had not abandoned us. We adopted this song as "our song." Whenever we heard it Terri squealed with excitement, "Momma, our song is playing on the radio." We were especially fond of the end of the song when the little girl said, "I love you mommy" and the mother said, "I love you too, sweetheart." As with most things, time has a way of making things better. We adjusted to our new lives, just the two of us.

Now it is too painful for me to listen to this song, especially the last verse, "when one of us is gone, and one of us is left to carry on." I never imagined God would leave me in this world to live without my beloved daughter.

After the divorce we were fortunate to have the love and support of her paternal grandparents, Roy and Cornelia. Terri spent the night with them every Saturday. Because I worked past the time the childcare closed, they picked her up in the afternoons. Terri loved food and she was always hungry. Her granddaddy enjoyed spoiling her, so he made not one but two sandwiches for her to eat as soon as she got in the car. He didn't want her to be hungry on the way home.

I called them anytime, day or night; they were always available to take care of her. She loved her grandmother and granddaddy and they adored her. Raising Terri without their support would have been impossible. Along with my parents, Roy and Cornelia were instrumental in molding her into the beautiful person she became.

4

CHURCH

When Terri was eight or nine years old, my Mom and oldest sister were sick. On Sunday mornings I would stay with them and prepare lunch for everyone while Terri and Daddy went to church. Momma and Daddy's house was close enough to the church so on nice mornings, they walked. I watched them from the kitchen window walking home hand in hand. She would bless the food and Daddy always said, "The good Lord hears that one."

The people at our church were wonderful with Terri. Since she could not keep up with the other children her age, her Sunday school teachers gave her one-on-one instruction. She came home telling me all about the stories of the bible.

She made the decision to accept Jesus as her personal Savior when she was nine years old. I wasn't there because I was at home with Momma and Linda. Daddy said no one coaxed her to go down front that morning. She went on her own and was crying as she went. I was so sad I missed such an important day in her life. However, our entire family attended her baptism. She was so pretty in her all-white dress. She held her nose tight as our preacher baptized her and wasn't even afraid.

Her intellectual disability did not prevent her from having a strong relationship with God. I admired her simple faith and wished my faith could be more like hers–so sweet and accepting without question. Throughout her life she prayed earnestly for anyone who needed prayer. If we were in the middle of Walmart or the grocery store, she would stop and say, "Momma, hold my hand and let's pray."

Years later when Momma and Linda had passed away and I had remarried, Terri became a member of our adult Sunday school class. She was an adult herself by then but only in age. Terri was adored by the other class members. They always made a big deal over her birthday, singing Happy Birthday and bringing her presents. Terri loved the attention and was grateful for the presents. "Thank you for my presents." When she was a kid I taught her good manners. She always said," thank you, yes sir, yes ma'am, and excuse me." People were astonished by her polite demeanor.

One Sunday morning, Larry, our teacher, was talking about all of the advances in technology. "We are living in an age where children have their very own cell phone," he said.

Terri was so serious when she held up her hand, "I don't have a cell phone." We all laughed and she laughed her beautiful laugh right along with us. She didn't have a cell phone because she wasn't able to use it. At home she had her own special phone programmed to dial the important people in her life. All she had to do was push the big button with their name on it. She never learned to read or write, yet she could recognize a few names.

In Sunday school and preaching she always sat beside me. She put her head on my shoulder and sometimes we held hands. Some of my fondest memories are the times we spent together in church. I can still feel her head on my shoulder and her hand in mine. It was a special place for Terri. One she looked forward to every week.

Terri, Girl Scout of the Year Award, age 7, 1979

5

GRAMMAR SCHOOL YEARS

Terri attended kindergarten at Erwin Elementary school without any special resources. The school system was spearheading a new concept in learning for kindergarten-age students called "an open classroom." Students didn't sit at a desk; they sat on the floor in a circle. Mrs. Breland, her teacher, was especially patient with her. It was a good year for us.

First grade was an entirely different story. The school psychologist tested Terri and placed her in a self-contained class for the Educable Mentally Handicapped. Her IQ was in the 50's range. An IQ of 70 or below is a low score and an indicator of an intellectual disability characterized by significant cognitive impairment. It was my first time to be clinically confronted with the depth of my child's mental disability–another heartbreaking step down the road of raising a child with special needs.

Terri's score placed her in the mild to moderate range, meaning her mind would always be a child's mind. She would learn to care for herself to some degree yet she would always require supervision. She would need special resources in school in a contained setting, meaning she attended classes with children more like herself. Her intellectual disability placed her at a higher risk for psychological problems. Every child is different in their challenges, needs, and talents regardless of their IQ score and Terri certainly was no exception to the rule.

On the first day of school, I couldn't help myself. I was standing in the hall with my back against the wall squalling like a baby. The mother of another special needs student tried to console me, but it didn't help. I bawled for weeks. At this point in time, Terri did not realize she was different. It would be several years later before she understood the meaning of "Special."

Terri's first grade teacher felt she should be placed in the Trainable Handicapped Class because she could not sit at a desk and was disruptive to the other students. She talked nonstop, continually repeating the same things. I talked with the school psychologist, yet she insisted Terri was properly placed. She was so cold and rude to me, I practically despised her. Fortunately Terri's teacher loved her dearly and worked hard to make the best of the situation.

For many years Terri got stuck on this one statement, "I have long blond hair, little arms and legs, and my Momma drives around in a Datsun B210." We thought she never would outgrow this chant, yet eventually she did. But several years later when she graduated from high school, her Uncle Wayne made sure we remembered it! He placed an ad in the local newspaper for Terri's graduation from high school. Included in the ad was a picture of her celebrating her birthday with her cousins (party hats and all) when they were young children. The caption read, "Congratulations Terri on your graduation from high school! We remember as if it were yesterday when you had long blond hair, little arms and legs, and rode around in a Datsun B210."

I slowly began to accept my child would not be like her cousin, Cameron. Her life would be entirely different. Sometimes I would stand at the window as she boarded her special needs bus for school and contemplate our future together. What would life hold for us?

Brokenhearted as I was, I was thankful her condition was not worse. I observed the children in the Physically Handicapped Class and thanked God Terri could run and play. Run and play she did. She had a Sit-N-Spin she spun around and around tirelessly. She had a Big Wheels bike she rode as well as any child her age. She had so much fun laughing and playing, at times I could almost fool myself in to thinking she was like any other child her age.

As a single parent I had to work full time. At night I helped Terri attempt to learn her ABC's and numbers. I was determined she would learn the basics. To some degree, I was still in denial. She wanted to please me and she would try so hard. The truth was she didn't have the intelligence to learn the basics. I needed emotional support and became good friends with the principal at Terri's self-contained school. She finally convinced me I was spinning my wheels. We should be doing fun things with our time together. I took her advice and gave up on the nightly drills of ABCs and numbers much to Terri's relief.

Terri's school was the only school in the county that was not air conditioned. I was President of the PTA and helped develop a plan to raise the money to have it installed. We held numerous fundraisers. My favorite was the Spring Fling. The main event was the announcement of King and Queen. Terri was crowned Queen. She was nine years old at the time. I can still see the look of glee on her face as she sat on the stage in her beautiful dress and wearing a tiara – the center of everyone's attention. Terri was the happiest when she was in the spotlight.

Terri went everywhere with me. I always said we were joined at the hip. I talked to her about everything. She learned the colors of red and green from the stop lights as we rode down

Main Street. We observed the different colors of cars and talked about road signs. She was really observant, especially when it came to recognizing cars. She never missed my car. If she were riding with someone else and saw my car parked at the office or grocery store, she couldn't wait to tell me about seeing it. Seeing my car was a big deal to Terri.

The school psychologist gave me credit for her advanced social skills. She never met a stranger and could remember you if she had only met you once. She was outgoing and fun to be around. She wasn't shy. She could walk into a room of strangers and before the evening was over she made her way around to everyone there introducing herself, "Hello, I'm Terri. I have a new radio." She even offered her new friends the opportunity to listen to it, but only for a few seconds. "Would you like to listen to my radio? That's long enough, give it back to me."

Wayne told me Terri would always have an attention-getting tactic up her sleeve and he was right. At his house she asked for Band-Aids for imaginary injuries. He kept an assortment of them on hand with her favorite characters in mind – Mickey and Minnie Mouse, Peter Pan, Barney – it wasn't unusual for her to be wearing several at a time.

She enjoyed playing the lost and found game when we went shopping. She pretended to be lost in the store. I always warned Terri about getting away from me before we went to the mall. I threatened all sorts of punishment when she pulled this little trick on me. After explaining the dangers and the consequences, she still jumped at the first chance she had to get out of my sight. She ran ahead of me and told the first person she came in contact with she was lost and couldn't find her mother. I often heard someone over the intercom calling me to come to the service desk. Sometimes they couldn't understand her and I heard all sorts of names, "Mrs. Bedbottom, your daughter is at the service desk, please come pick her up."

Like most kids, she played hide and seek under the clothes rack. I would frantically look everywhere for her. I knew when she was in a hiding place because I wouldn't get a call to come to the service desk. I looked until I found her. As she got older, she outgrew the lost and found game.

Congratulations, Terri Ledbetter, upon your graduation! We remember as if it were yesterday when you had long blond hair, little arms & legs, and road around in a Datsun B210.

Left to right — Elizabeth, Cameron, Terri, Chris. This ad was placed in our local newspaper by Uncle Wayne when Terri graduated from High School in 1993

6

CHALLENGES

Because of my income, I qualified for a subsidized Farmers Home Loan. Terri was seven or eight years old when we moved into our very own new home with three bedrooms and one-and-one-half baths. The truth be known, Terri qualified for the free lunch program at school. I had too much pride and only owned one tube of lipstick so she could take her lunch money to school every Monday morning. She had two pairs of jeans and several tops. I kept her jeans washed and dressed her neat and clean every day. Momma gave Terri her cousin's hand-me-down clothes and bought every Easter dress she ever owned as a child. We loved each other and our new home.

If you are reading this book and the parent or caregiver of a special needs child, you understand the challenges involved in protecting and training our children. We soon learned our neighborhood left much to be desired. There was an older man who lived across the street from us. Terri called him Paw-Paw like the other kids in the neighborhood, yet for some reason I had a gut feeling this man could not be trusted. My suspicions were confirmed when Terri told me he asked to see her breasts. I never allowed her to go near him again.

If dirty old men were not enough to deal with, there were mean kids in the neighborhood. The kids across the street told Terri she was retarded. She didn't know what retarded meant, yet she knew it wasn't a compliment. They made fun of her special needs school and taunted her because she could not read and write. She came home bawling her eyes out. I told her to ignore them, but the damage was done. She was heartbroken, her innocence shattered. She spent hours sitting at the table in the den trying her best to write. She wanted desperately to prove the mean kids wrong.

What parents of other children can easily accomplish, it is a task of monumental effort for us and our children. When Terri was between the ages of nine and seventeen we went to the Saluda Center for counseling. Her therapist stressed the importance of training her to become more independent.

One of the first things we tackled was teaching her to sleep in her own bed. When her daddy and I divorced, I allowed her to sleep with me. She said her prayer and I tucked her in and kissed her goodnight in her own bed around 9 o'clock every night. Later when I went to bed, she came sneaking in my room and crawled up next to me. This had been going on for quite some time so we knew it would be a difficult habit for her to break. The therapist suggested I lock her in her room. "Are you crazy? I can't lock my child in her room." Then he suggested I lock myself in my room to prevent her from getting in my bed. "No, I am afraid she will go outside screaming and wake up the neighborhood." He told me it was a chance I would need to take.

On the first night of the new routine I explained to Terri she was too big to be sleeping in the same bed with her mother. My fears were realized when I locked myself in my room. She went outside screaming. It was torturous for me, but I did not unlock my door and remained in my room. She eventually came in the house and went to bed. Night two wasn't much better; she sat outside my room begging me to unlock my door. I stayed true to the behavior plan and did not respond to her or unlock my door. Once total exhaustion set in, she gave up and went to her bed. It felt like a lifetime, yet it was two to three weeks before she was able to sleep in her bed. We reached our goal, yet it was hard on both of us.

We continued to see the therapist, yet I didn't always agree with him. Since Terri looked perfectly normal, he sometimes assumed she could accomplish more than she was capable of. He couldn't understand why she wasn't bathing herself or washing her hair. Parents know their children better than anyone. It's our responsibility to decide what is best for them.

For many years Terri attended Special Olympics. The games are held in April of each year. Sometimes the weather cooperated and it was a beautiful spring day, other times it was cold or raining for the event

One year stands out in my mind. It was an ideal day to be outside; Terri was in line for the 100 meter dash. I was standing close to the finish line where several coaches were stationed. I overheard one of the coaches yelling across the field, "Get that girl off of the track. She can't run with a special needs athlete." He was talking about Terri. She looked like any other child and no one could tell she was intellectually challenged until she began telling you about her headphone radio or latest watch. Once I realized he was talking about Terri, I went over and explained the situation. When the race began and she lagged behind the other athletes her condition was obvious.

I cheered her on until she reached the finish line, "Run Terri, run baby, you can do it." It never bothered Terri if she did not win. She was thrilled to be participating. Regardless if she placed, she was a champion in my heart.

When she was older, she lost interest in the games and wouldn't attend. By that time she had developed migraine headaches; bright lights, loud noises, and crowds bothered her.

7

SPECIAL TIMES

As an insurance agent for a local insurance company, I qualified for annual sales conventions. One summer when Terri was eight years old we went to Walt Disney World. Her grandmother, Cornelia, went with us to Florida so she could take care of her while I attended convention events.

I didn't want to drive, so we took the Amtrak. When the train rolled into the station with its loud whistle, Terri began to scream. Everyone was staring. There was no way to silence her. She didn't calm down until the whistle quit blowing. Once we boarded the train, she slept the entire way to Florida.

It was in the middle of summer and really hot at Disney World. The lines at Magic Kingdom were long. She was so impatient. Waiting in line was hard for her. She complained constantly about the heat and long lines. I remember one of the tourists asked me what was wrong with my daughter. It was a difficult day for all of us.

When it cooled down in late evening we lined Main Street, U.S.A. with hundreds of other people to watch for the parade. She was in a much better mood. She was absolutely mesmerized as the Electric Light Parade rolled by. I will never forget the look of wonder on her face. It made the entire trip worthwhile. The fireworks over Cinderella Castle were another one of her favorite attractions. As were all of the Disney characters, with Mickey and Minnie Mouse being her favorites.

Another time we went to Washington, DC. Since we had already experienced a train ride, we decided to fly. With Terri you always knew there would be something to upset her, like the loud whistle of Amtrak, yet it was hard to anticipate what it might be. On this trip she was wearing her headphone radio and carrying her favorite doll as we approached the gate at the airport. There was no way she was going to put her doll on the conveyor belt and let it be eaten up by the thing with waving arms. She started screaming. The line was backing up and people were staring. I begged the baggage officer to let her walk through the gate with her doll. She refused. I had to yank Terri's doll out of her arms, throw it on the conveyor belt, and drag her through the gate screaming. When we got on the other side, she was so relieved to find her doll intact; she latched on to it for dear life. I wondered what else could go terribly wrong before we landed in DC. She was a perfect angel on the plane; much to my relief she loved flying.

Sightseeing didn't excite her. The Washington Monument or Lincoln Memorial didn't hold any meaning for her. The highlight of her trip was eating out every meal. She wasn't afraid of the baggage official on the way back home. She was so proud as she placed her doll on the conveyor belt to be x-rayed, "I am not afraid, Momma."

Another convention took us to St. Louis, Missouri. A trip to the top of the Gateway Arch wasn't on our agenda. Terri would have gladly gone. It was me. I am afraid of heights and couldn't muster the courage to go. She enjoyed the flight out there and back and as always the highlight of her trip was dining at fancy restaurants.

Since Carowinds Amusement Park is practically in our back yard, we visited the park often. Getting soaked on the River Rapids thrilled her. She also enjoyed splashing the day away in the Water Park. She liked pontoon boat rides on the Catawba River with friends. She never learned to swim, yet I taught her to doggie paddle. She had a tremendous respect for the water and I made certain she wore her life jacket.

Trips to Springmaid Beach or Ocean Isle with the extended family were annual events for many years. One year, Doc, my husband, Terri, and I were wading out in the ocean when a huge wave knocked us down. Thank God we were all holding hands. Doc and I hung on tight to Terri as the undercurrent pulled us down. She came up coughing and sputtering. She never wanted to go in the ocean again. We settled for walks on the beach from then on.

Par 3 golf was a favorite sport for our family when vacationing on Ocean Isle. Aunt Molly and Terri followed along with us on one of our golf outings. Terri decided to rest and sat down in a bed of fire ants. In no time her legs were covered in ants and she was screaming hysterically. We all tried to get them off of her as fast as we could. Needless to say, she was stung all over her legs. Aunt Molly recommended Gold Bond powder to relieve the pain.

In spite of some kind of episode involving Terri, these times remained special for our family and didn't hamper our enjoyment overall.

Doc, Momma, Scott, and Terri, 1993

8

HIGH SCHOOL YEARS

Terri stayed in grammar school until she was 14 years old. I liked having her in a self-contained school because it was small and we felt safe there. Because of her age, the principal decided it was time for her to move up. She stayed in junior high for one year. It was a nightmare. Her teacher had family issues and was out for the majority of the school year. Terri didn't like change and didn't take to a different substitute teacher every day. She cried and begged to go home. Of course, this was disruptive to the other students. For this reason she spent much of her time in detention, commonly referred to as the "Box" for the majority of the year. Junior high wasn't for Terri. Faith was a long-time Trainable Mentally Handicapped teacher at the high school. The next year Terri went into her class. She blossomed under Faith's direction. More emphasis was placed on life skills and less on academic skills. Life was good again.

One of the highlight's of Terri's high school years was the prom. Tim, her classmate, was her date for the evening. She was absolutely gorgeous in her prom dress. We didn't go in search for a dress because she never liked to shop unless it was for something with a Disney character on it. She was happy with the clothes I bought and laid out for her to wear every day. She wore the same dress she had worn in my and Doc's wedding. It had a floral bodice with a matching green skirt and fell just below the knees with shoes to match. It was worn off the shoulders. She wore a pearl necklace with pearl earrings. A close friend styled her hair and did her makeup. In my eyes she was the most beautiful girl on earth.

Tim was so handsome in his black tuxedo. I had filled his Mom in on the details of Terri's dress so she could rent a matching vest for him. Since Terri's dress was worn off the shoulders, he bought her a wrist corsage. My twin sister was the camera bug in our family. She took a picture of Terri and Tim in every pose imaginable.

My husband and I, along with Terri's grandmother, took them out to dinner at Tim's favorite Chinese restaurant and then dropped them off at the school. The event was well chaperoned. Terri told me they danced the entire evening. They were exhausted when they arrived back at our house. Both of them plopped down on the sofa and dozed as they waited for Tim's mother to pick him up. I was so happy for her. She felt like all the other girls at school. For just a little while she was not different.

When she was in high school she was plagued with ingrown toe nails. She spent more time in an orthopedic boot than she did a regular shoe. The surgeon told me he had to give her an unusual amount of anesthesia to operate on her toe. Looking back on it, this was probably an early indication Terri was getting sick. I promised her a pink radio if she let the surgeon operate. She was so brave–willing to do anything for a pink radio.

Terri's paternal grandfather passed away when she was 16. She wasn't new to the experience of death. We had lost my mother a couple of years earlier after a long illness. It was different when her grandfather died. She was in a state of shock the morning of his death. She did not cry. She appeared to be in a daze. When she saw him in the casket she screamed. We all rushed over to her. "Terri, are you alright?"

"Yes, I'm okay, I'm okay," yet I knew she was struggling to keep it together. She was quiet as we rode the sixty miles to the cemetery. They had always been so close. She had gone with him to the flea market every Saturday morning. Later they would go to a nearby grill for a hamburger. She loved her grand-daddy and he thought the sun rose and set for her.

9

FALSE ALLEGATIONS

Terri spent hours at a time in her swing; she talked and talked imagining all sorts of things. She spent so much time in her swing she rubbed red places on the backs of her legs, so her grandmother made her a cushion to sit on. She was religious about taking it to the swing with her, yet she wasn't able to place it so her legs were protected.

I was surprised and furious to learn her gym teacher reported us to Social Services for abuse. Of course, the social worker from Social Services knew the red marks were from the swing and not abuse. Terri was impressionable, meaning she was easily influenced. After her teacher asked her several times if she had been spanked, Terri finally said she had. I realize it's a teacher's responsibility to report suspected abuse so I let it go the first time.

A second time the same teacher reported her to Social Services, once again for the red marks. I went to the school to talk with her. She refused to believe the marks were from the swing. "Janice, I have known you since you were in high school; I know you are not the person responsible for those marks. I do believe you are covering up for someone." She was defensive, wanting to know how I knew she was the person who made the report.

"Terri came home and told me, how else would I know? Why didn't you talk with me first? I could have easily explained the marks. I would never allow anyone to abuse my child." I was so upset; I felt my hair standing on ends. "I can't believe you had Terri strip down naked and made pictures of her. Don't you realize how demoralizing this can be to a child, especially one who doesn't grasp the situation?" The social worker had shown me the pictures. I was livid.

Once again, Social Services found the allegations to be unfounded. The teacher finally came to the conclusion Terri was not spanked. Parents of special needs children have enough to deal with without interference from people who do not understand our children.

Another time while she was in high school, I received a phone call to come to the school. She was in the principal's office, shaking all over and crying her heart out. "What's wrong baby?" The principal did not give Terri an opportunity to speak. He immediately went into a tirade about her behavior. The school resource officer was in the office and added her two cents worth to the conversation. I told them I would need to talk with my daughter's teacher. Faith came to the office and as I suspected Terri was having a bad day. Some days she was upset for no apparent reason and this was one of those days. The school resource officer and principal had overreacted and escalated the situation. When she refused to go to the office, the principal began dragging her down the hall toward his office. At that point she was petrified and started screaming.

Cameron, her cousin, heard the turmoil from his classroom. It was exam day and he had completed his exam. He asked to be excused, "That's my cousin, I can help."

"Please do what you can to help that poor child," the teacher said.

Cameron got down on the floor with Terri and talked with her until she calmed down enough so he could walk her to the office. "Who is that boy?" the principal asked.

"He's my cousin," Terri said.

Joyce and I spent a lot of time together when our children were small so Cameron and Terri were very close.

"Cameron knows how to treat Terri with kindness and respect," I said.

"I want that boy's schedule. I want to know where he is every minute of the day in the event we need him again," the principal said.

After letting the principal and security guard know how displeased I was with their behavior, I took Terri home so she could calm down.

Cameron was upset because of the way the principal and security guard had treated his cousin. The next day he and some of his friends went to the principal's office to inform him they did not agree with the school's disciplinary policy and it definitely should not apply to a special needs student.

Cameron had always been Terri's guardian angel. He looked out for her in daycare and his protection continued through the years. Whenever he was around, he came to her rescue.

Terri and Cameron, 2008

Terri at Mom and Doc's wedding, 1990

10

REMARRIAGE

I remarried when Terri was 18 years old. I had been dating Doc for five years and he was good to us. I remember asking her permission to marry him and she was all for it. At the time, she didn't realize that sharing me with someone else wouldn't always be easy for her. Doc and I were married at Joyce and Wayne's house. It was a gorgeous outdoor wedding on a spring day in May. It was May 26, 1990, to be exact, three days after I turned 40.

Our children were in the wedding. Doc's son Scott was the best man. His daughter Tessa and Terri were bridesmaids. Terri was stunning in her green dress and straw bonnet. She had a good relationship with her stepsister and stepbrother. Though she was a little jealous of Scott because he could drive a car and she couldn't. She often asked me, "Momma, I am older than Scott, why can he drive a car and I can't?"

I tried to help her understand, "Terri, you know how nervous you get at times. You wouldn't want to have a wreck and get hurt or hurt someone else." She always accepted my explanations. Years earlier daddy had taught me how to turn Terri's thinking around. He advised, "Don't allow her to obsess over negative things." He was a wise man.

Doc was a good stepfather. He was stricter than I could be and more of a disciplinarian. It made for a good balance and Terri was the beneficiary. Life was good; at least we thought it was.

The first year Doc and I were married, we decided to sell our homes and build a new one. We didn't want to live in his house or mine, we wanted our home. We built a two-story with Terri in mind. Her bedroom was upstairs and ours was downstairs. We designed an open balcony to the den so she would not be isolated from us. She had her own sitting room, yet she didn't spend much time in it. She was content to follow me everywhere I went in the house. My husband said that would drive him crazy, yet it never bothered me. It was time we could spend together. I can still see her sitting in one dinette chair with her feet propped up on another chair watching me cook the evening meal on Sundays. If I was making deviled eggs, she always wanted to lick the spoon and plate. She was another pair of hands and legs helping with the chores. One of her jobs was putting the laundry away once I had washed it.

She would sit at my feet every time I took a break to rest in my rocking chair. Even today it is one of my most treasured memories of Terri, sitting there on the floor–sometimes quietly and sometimes talking away, but always there.

Much to our surprise Terri couldn't make the adjustment to the new house. We noticed she did not want to go with us to see the progress when it was being built. She would rather stay at home and swing. We also realized she was upset more often. She threw her jam box on the cement sidewalk and broke it for no apparent reason. When we made the move from the old house to the new house, she could not sleep. Every night for weeks I took her to her grandmother's house. Since nothing had changed there she went straight to bed and instantly fell asleep.

11

ILLNESS

Not long after moving into the new house, Terri came home from school and told me she did not want to live anymore. I knew something was terribly wrong. I made her an appointment with our primary care physician. He referred us to a psychiatrist. We did not have a good experience with this doctor. When I explained her symptoms, he kept saying, "Oh, me. Oh, my." I wanted to slap his face. He acted as if her case was hopeless. He prescribed an antipsychotic medication. I gave it to her hoping it would make her feel better. It did not; instead, she became worse so I stopped giving it to her.

After three weeks of going back and forth with Terri to her grandmother's house to sleep, I decided it was time for her to stay home and sleep in her own bed. It was a Sunday night; she threw a fit, packed a bag of clothes and left walking. "Momma, I'm leaving. I'm going to my grandmother's house."

I coaxed her back in the house before she got past the entrance way to our neighborhood. Desperate for help, I called the probate judge, a friend of the family. He told me most of the people he knew who went to this particular psychiatrist became worse instead of better. He recommended she go to the Baptist

Hospital in Columbia. A referral was made the next day. We were told to expect a hospital stay and to bring her clothes. My daddy, my husband, and I traveled to Columbia with Terri. She wanted to go, she knew she needed help. What she didn't understand was a hospital stay meant she would be away from me.

She was admitted to the psychiatric unit. This hospital stay would not be like any other hospital stay. I could not be with her, she would be alone–a terrifying experience for her. I was so upset because I was leaving her with strangers in a strange place, behind locked doors. Terri was frantic, screaming and crying for her mother. Leaving her behind that night was one of the hardest things I had ever done in my life.

I was allowed to visit her every day except for one day each week. I called her every morning and drove 60 miles to visit every night except for the forbidden night of Tuesday. I was distraught to say the least.

A social worker was assigned to us. We got off to a terrible start though our relationship changed after she learned more about us. She said, "Didn't you know getting married in Terri's teenage years could make her sick?"

I was totally blown away, "Are you crazy? I would have never gotten married if I thought there was even a slight chance my daughter could become sick." At this point I was hysterical myself. How dare she suggest I was responsible for Terri's illness? I believe in my heart she was going to become sick regardless of my decision to get married. Her traumatic birth played a role in my opinion. Of course, I will never know with certainty.

The social worker asked me about the scratches on the back of her neck. I explained I had noticed them and questioned Terri about them. She told me another student in her class had scratched her. As it turned out, she was scratching herself. She thought gnats were bothering her (hallucinations). I was told this was a sign of a psychotic episode. I don't have the words to explain my fear and regrets. Why had I not seen this coming? I blamed myself. Thinking back on it there were signs. Terri had become withdrawn, spending more time in her swing. She couldn't sleep. She had outbursts for no reason. I asked the social worker why God gave children like Terri to me. I wasn't a psychologist. I didn't know or understand the warning signs. All I knew was I loved her with all of my heart and soul.

She was released from the hospital after three weeks. Her doctor told me she would eventually adjust to her new home. It was some time before she completely made the adjustment; yet, when she did, she loved it. She often said, "Momma, I love my new house!"

Family therapy was recommended and a therapist was assigned to us. We went to see her once a week. As Terri's condition improved the time between sessions extended to two weeks, then three weeks, and finally once a month.

When she came home from the hospital, she was so heavily sedated she couldn't decide if she wanted to go up or come down the stairs. The social worker told me she would be on medication for the rest of her life. The diagnosis was schizophrenia. There is not a clearly defined test that proves the diagnosis, yet her symptoms were a strong indicator this was the case. It is a chronic and severe mental disorder. Delusions (false beliefs) and hallucinations (seeing or hearing things other people do not see or hear) are the most common symptoms. Terri experienced hallucinations and other symptoms such as depression, anxiety, and sleep problems.

According to the National Institute of Mental Health schizophrenia usually strikes between the ages of 16 and 30. The prevalence of the disease in the U.S. ranges between 0.25% and 0.64%. It presents an increased risk of premature mortality (death at a younger age than the general population). Medical conditions such as heart disease, liver disease, and diabetes contribute to the higher premature mortality rate. (https://www.nimh.nih.gov/health/topics/schizophrenia/index.shtml, accessed June 12, 2019).

The illness is manageable with proper medication and treatment. Terri received the best medical treatment and the support of a loving family. She never had a relapse. I take great pride in this accomplishment.

I recently came across a card I sent to Terri when she was in the hospital. The front cover is a verse written by Helen Steiner Rice, *"The Lord is our salvation and our strength in every fight, our redeemer and protector, our eternal guiding light . . . He has promised to sustain us, He's our refuge from all harms, and underneath this refuge are His everlasting arms!"* The inside verse reads, *"His arms are strong enough to carry you until you can stand on firm ground again. May you feel His closeness and His love."* My note to Terri reads, *"I'm so happy the medication is helping you feel better. I'm proud of you for realizing you needed help and for being brave enough to go to the hospital. You really are becoming quite a young lady. I love you very much."* Momma.

It was rough going when she first came home from the hospital. We were told to lock her in her room when she was disruptive or out of control. To keep her in her room we had to remove the door knob on her side of the door. It tore my heart out, but I followed the therapist's orders because I desperately wanted her to get better so our lives could resume some form of normalcy.

The first night she was home, she cried and wanted to go to her grandmother's house.

I said, "No."

She then became belligerent; I had to lock her in her room. She pitched a fit and tore up her blinds. I can't tell you how difficult it was for me and Doc to endure her rages. Our therapist told me to make her pay for the blinds out of her own money. She never tore them up again.

Her behavior placed a huge strain on our marriage. I remember asking Doc to take a walk with me on the night before she was released from the hospital. I explained to him, in no uncertain terms, Terri was my child, she needed me and I would always be there for her. Doc had not bargained for all of this when we married. He became withdrawn and every day after work he went upstairs to watch TV by himself. After about three weeks of this behavior, I went upstairs slung open the door and told him if he wanted our marriage to survive, he would go to family counseling with me and Terri. Later that night he came downstairs and agreed to go. Thank God for our therapist because I truly don't believe we would have made it without her guidance.

Gradually Terri came to realize we meant business. We were not going to tolerate her disruptive behaviors. Life was returning to normal again. I was determined to help her get back to where she was before all this happened and for the most part she did. She suffered with occasional episodes of hallucinations, thinking gnats were bothering her, for the rest of her life. Sometimes I saw scratches on her arms and legs when I bathed her. We tried So Soft Avon lotion for the gnats telling her it would make them go away. We tried everything we could think of to make life better for her.

A few months after her release from the hospital, it was decided she would be a good candidate for Clozaril, a fairly new medication for people with schizophrenia. It was promoted as a miracle drug. It can cause serious and sometimes fatal infections. For this reason the drug was only available from a certified pharmacy and required ongoing blood work before it could be dispensed. Terri received her medication by mail from CVS pharmacy in Columbia. The required blood tests were administered by her GP. Initially we went every week, then every two weeks, then three weeks, and eventually once a month. She was so brave – never afraid of a little ole needle stick.

The list of side effects for Clozaril was endless. Yet I knew if Terri was going to have any quality of life, she would need to take this drug. She certainly fared better with it than she had with other medications. She wasn't as sedated. One of its most troubling side effects was headaches. She had horrible migraines. Sometimes she may have as many as three episodes in a week. We never knew when they were going to strike. The only way she could feel better was to take a sleeping pill, go to bed and sleep the headache off. Again we had to resort to locking her in her room to get her to lie down. Otherwise, she would constantly ask for another pill. We would tell her, "Terri, we can't give you another pill, lie down, you will feel better once the pill gets in your system."

She would beg for a pill, "Momma, give me another pill. I want a pill, give me a pill . . . "

Several times we were at a restaurant in Charlotte and we were forced to come home without eating our meal because she suddenly became ill. When she was sick, Doc or I stayed at home with her. I often said to her, "Terri, I am so sorry you are sick."

She could see my pain, "It's OK, Momma, it's not your fault."

Most people never realized Terri was sick, they only saw her when she was well and her happy self. My baby was sick and it broke my heart.

Her doctor tried several medications to alleviate her headaches. Imitrex didn't work because she couldn't tell when a headache was coming on. Depakote didn't have much if any effect. Finally, Topamax worked. Her headaches didn't go away completely, yet they were far less frequent and not as severe when they did occur. Hallalujah!

Other side effects for Clozaril were trembling hands and increased salivation. The salivation was especially bothersome. She had to place a towel over her pillow at night.

After her illness she became a creature of habit going to bed when it got dark–winter, spring, summer, or fall. Each year the time change threw her for a loop especially in the summer months. Waiting on it to get dark so she could go to bed was hard for her.

Many people with emotional disorders do not take their medications. We were fortunate because Terri wanted to take her medicine. So much so she obsessed over it, "Where is my medicine? Where is my medicine?"

Doc suggested we put her pills in a weekly pill box. Much to our relief she quit stressing over her medication. It comforted her to know it was ready and waiting for her.

Terri didn't allow intellectual challenges or schizophrenia to define her life. She suffered through the bad days and made the most of the good days. She didn't feel sorry for herself or complain. I will forever marvel at her courage and strength.

12

LIFE AFTER GRADUATION FROM HIGH SCHOOL

Terri graduated from High School in 1993. I was full of pride as she walked across the stage to receive her certificate. I cried. Since she was a special needs student, she was allowed to stay in high school until she was 21. It had been a long fifteen years in the school system with a lot of up and downs. Her step-brother, Scott, was three years younger, yet he was graduating the same year. We honored both of them with a dinner at Nogie's Restaurant–family, close friends, and teachers were invited to help us celebrate.

Since college wasn't an option for her, she attended the day program at the local Disabilities and Special Needs Board. She was assigned a job coach and worked at the Convalescent Center washing and folding clothes for a short period of time. It didn't work out because her motor skills weren't good enough for her to neatly fold clothes. At home her job was to put the clothes away after I had washed and folded them.

Our dream of her having a job out in the community would not be realized because she continued a pattern of disruptive behavior at times (mostly when she had a headache). This did not mean she was violent. Terri was never violent. She would sit in the floor and cry for her momma, "I want my momma, I want my momma . . . ."

The psychologist at the workshop arranged a timeout area for her. It was a secluded and quiet place where Terri could rest and get herself calmed down.

Terri remained in the sheltered workshop for the rest of her life. The van picked her up at 8 in the morning and brought her home around 2:30 every afternoon Monday through Friday of each week. She often came home complaining, "Momma, I hate our dilapidated van. It is always breaking down." One time it caught on fire. She was really upset about that. I remember telling her if I had the money I would buy her a new van. Shortly after she passed away the center bought three new vans. A new van would have made her a happy girl. It was bittersweet for me. I was glad the center had them, yet sad because Terri wasn't here to ride in a new van.

At the workshop there were contracts for the adults to work on–simple jobs but ones that gave them a sense of accomplishment. One contract was collegiate flags you see flying from car windows. Other contracts included stuffing envelopes and putting stems in glass Christmas balls. Terri worked with the laundry crew for many years. Her favorite part of this job was delivering freshly washed and ironed napkins and table clothes to local restaurants. She loved cutting up with the owners at the various business establishments they serviced.

The workshop gave Terri purpose. She got dressed every morning like other people and went to work. She looked forward to going to the workshop because she had friends there. Andy was her boyfriend and they were inseparable. She enjoyed socializing with her friends. The workshop was an important element in her life and necessary for her mental well-being.

13

ACCEPTING HER PLACE IN SOCIETY

Terri was beginning to accept her place in society. She would say, "Momma, I am special."

"Yes, you are sweetheart and I love you just the way God made you."

Terri never did learn to take a bath on her own, though we tried really hard. I thought maybe she just wouldn't do it for me. One summer I hired a college student majoring in Special Education to teach her personal hygiene skills. Terri worked hard at it, but it wasn't in the cards. I bathed her, brushed her teeth, styled her hair, and laid out her clothes every morning of her life. She was so sweet, "Thank you, Momma, for washing my hair." She was grateful for everything you did for her, no matter how big or small.

My friend, Terry, said Terri left a handprint on the heart of every person she touched. Jimmie, said she left a footprint on her heart. For my friend Shirley, it was love at first sight. When she met Terri, she wrote me the sweetest card telling me how much she enjoyed meeting her.

We went to Mane Street Hair Designers for our hair care. The girls at the shop loved Terri and looked forward to her coming. Debbie styled my hair while Lisa styled Terri's. As I mentioned earlier, she loved to dance so Debbie always stopped what she was doing to "get down" to the music on the radio with her. A trip to the beauty shop was a special treat for Terri.

A Sunday school class member recently reminded me of something Terri had a habit of saying. She said she would never forget her saying "Ain't that right, Momma?" She would be telling someone about her radio or latest watch and she would say to me, "Ain't that right, Momma?"

I would say, "Yes, sweetheart, that's right."

I am reminded of anther time in church when she told on me. I was wearing a wig and didn't want anyone to know. I told her before we went not to mention my wig. As soon as we sat down, she looked around at the people behind us, "Momma is wearing a wig." That was Terri; don't mention it to her if you didn't want it broadcast to the world. I could write a book about all the times she unknowingly embarrassed me, though I loved her just the same.

She added a spark to every get together. Sunday nights were special because we always had friends over for dinner. She loved to greet our guests. She ran to the front door, "Come on in Jeffy and Angela and make yourselves at home." It wasn't uncommon for her to have special names for people, like Jeffy for Jeff and Julie for his mother Judy. She loved to show off her room. Of course, I didn't allow her to take anyone in her room if I had not had the time to inspect it. I feared what they may find. She had a bad habit of throwing her dirty clothes in the floor. I didn't want our guests to see panties lying in the floor.

*Parker, the baby is Chucky, Seneca, Layla and Terri in the background,
Halloween, 2013*

14

WHAT MADE TERRI THE HAPPIEST?

I haven't told you much about what made Terri the happiest. Her birthday was her favorite day of the year. She was always telling everyone about it. She began the day after her birthday saying, "I have a birthday coming, December 16th." It was such a big deal for her. It is one of the things people remember the most about her. She asked for the same cake every year–a chocolate Coke-a-Cola cake. She was so predictable.

We always celebrated by going to a restaurant of her choice for dinner. We kept it low-key because she was prone to migraine headaches if she got over-excited. For this reason, only family and closest friends were invited. One year, she got so excited she missed her own birthday party. When Terri was happy, her laughter was music to my ears, because that wasn't always the case.

She loved her headphone radio; it went everywhere she went for her entire adult life. It was her security blanket. We tried unsuccessfully to graduate her up to a MP3 player or an IPOD. She refused to give up her old faithful radio. Christmas presents included enough batteries to last her the entire year.

She wanted to constantly change batteries, so we limited her to one a day. She thought it was new, she didn't know we were recycling them. We had to keep them hidden, because if she found her stash of batteries she would constantly change them. She could hardly wait for her battery every day, repeating over and over, "I want a new battery, Momma; I want a new battery, Momma." She was so impatient. I must admit, at times Doc and I lost our patience with her. We were good parents, yet far from perfect. I regret the times I didn't have enough patience.

She was a natural dancer. She knew the words to her favorite songs. She sang along with each song as she danced with the happiest expression on her face. Michael Jackson was her favorite artist. We were always dancing around the house to *Billie Jean* and *Thriller*. She was so full of life. We had so many good times. I thought they would last forever.

Even when she was older she spent hours in her swing. So much so, she rubbed red places on the back of her legs. I told you earlier about how much trouble that got us in.

She loved watches and headbands. Her favorite color was pink. She was always asking for a pink watch. We had to give up the headbands when she had an episode of head lice.

We taught her not to hug people or let anyone try on her headphones after the lice invasion. We were at the optometrist having her eye glasses repaired when we ran into Doctor Still and his wife. He had retired and hadn't seen Terri in quite some time so he immediately came toward her with his arms open to hug her. I remember Doctor Still's expression when Terri held up her hands and said, "I don't hug."

I said, "Terri, it's Okay to hug Doctor Still."

He stopped dead in his tracks, "It's okay, Janice, I understand." I didn't get a chance to explain because Terri was busy talking by then. I couldn't help but wonder what he was thinking.

One year she asked Santa Claus to bring her a pink bicycle. She was grown at the time and pink bicycles were hard to find for adults. My husband and I did not give up until we found one. On Christmas morning she rode it down the street and pushed it back up the hill. When she was a kid she could ride her bicycle as well as any other kid, but living on a hill and being out of shape was not on her side. She decided riding her bicycle was too much like work and never rode it again.

Holidays were special days for Terri. She loved to socialize so gathering with family and friends made her happy. Every year for Valentine's Day I bought her a huge valentine balloon, a heart-shaped box of candy, and gave her a special card. Easter included a new outfit for church and an Easter basket made especially for her by Aunt Joyce. We celebrated every July 4th with a hamburger and hot dog cookout. Dessert had to be homemade banana ice cream–everyone's favorite. A low country shrimp boil was the norm for Labor Day. She dressed as a witch on Halloween for many years. It was her favorite costume. We usually went to Joyce's house and Terri helped give out Halloween candy to the trick-or-treaters. As I said before she loved to eat and looked forward to the big Thanksgiving meal at Aunt Joyce and Uncle Wayne's house every year. Christmas was her favorite holiday. She couldn't wait to show everyone what Santa Claus had brought her when we met with the Steele family for our traditional family get-to-gather. Our friends, Marge and George, brought her an arm full of Christmas presents every Christmas. I have so many fond memories of her sitting in the floor in the den opening all of those presents– presents just for her. For every holiday (even St Patrick's Day) she could count on Aunt Joyce to send her a card. Included in the card would be a recent picture of her. Joyce treated Terri like her own child.

She was crazy about anything with Mickey Mouse on it. She

had several Mickey Mouse watches and a closet full of Mickey Mouse hoodies and sweat shirts. Her Christmas present every year from Uncle Wayne was a gift from the Disney Store.

Terri looked forward to every meal. While eating lunch she would ask, "Momma, what's for supper?" She liked most foods with the exception of corn bread. We often went to the Wagon Wheel restaurant after church for their Sunday buffet. She didn't mean to, but she made a mess with her food, spilling it all down the front of her clothes and on the floor. We always asked for extra napkins. At home we had a special place mat just for her. You could always tell where she sat because there was food all around her plate, on her chair, and on the floor. At Thanksgiving Uncle Wayne covered her chair with a towel. We never made a big deal about it. She would apologize, "Momma, I'm sorry; I don't mean to be so messy."

She wasn't a fan of TV, yet she loved to watch America's Funniest Videos on Sunday nights. She would laugh hysterically. To say Terri was excitable was an understatement. Her expression was unique to her–her cheeks flushed and her eyes opened wide as she placed her hands in front of her mouth, rubbed them rapidly up and down with a spark of joy and loud squeal of laughter.

Terri's unique expression of excitement, April, 2015

Terri and George, Christmas 2007

15

ESCALATOR EPISODE

Terri was around thirty five years old when we had the scare of our lives. It was Easter and Terri needed a new dress for church. On Saturday we went to Carolina Place in Pineville to shop for the perfect outfit. After what seemed like hours of searching, we found it–a green floral print two-piece ensemble. She looked pretty as a picture in her new outfit. She never did like to shop–the latest styles didn't matter to her. The only way I could get her to go was to promise her a nice meal afterwards. We were relieved to have accomplished our mission and ready to go to the restaurant for dinner. We had not eaten lunch and we were starving.

We had been riding escalators for as long as I can remember. It was never a problem–hop on and hop off. This day proved to be different. As we approached the escalator a nice lady motioned us ahead of her. I always cautioned Terri to be careful and step on a whole step. Maybe the nice lady caused her to feel a little rushed. She stepped on the escalator and only caught a part of the step. As the escalator ascended it threw her backwards. As it continued to move upwards, her head was bobbing up and down. She was screaming, "Momma, Momma!"

Her eyes were big as saucers. I went into panic mode and started yelling for someone to stop the escalator. The nice lady was able to press the stop button. When it finally stopped, I was trying to get Terri up. The contents of my purse spilled out and down the steps. Our screams were heard over the entire store. When I looked up a large group of people had crowded around the bottom of the escalator looking to see what had happened.

A store manager was immediately at our side. He didn't want me to move her until we evaluated her condition. She wasn't complaining of any pain, so together we sat her up. We then discovered her elbow was cut and she was bleeding. The cut was serious enough to require stitches. After completing the necessary paperwork involved in reporting an accident, we drove over to the emergency room at Mercy South.

We signed in at approximately 4 p.m. It was midnight when she was finally stitched up and released. A wait long enough to upset anyone, needless to say, Terri was beside herself. "When's the doctor coming Momma? I'm hungry. When's the doctor coming, Momma? I'm hungry." It was extremely hard for her to wait that long. I kept promising her it wouldn't be much longer. Somehow we managed to survive. After leaving the hospital we found an IHOP open. Pancakes never tasted so good.

After the escalator episode, we became "elevator girls." To this day, I will not ride an escalator. My friends lose their patience with me. They tell me I need to overcome my phobia. I tell them they didn't see the look of fear on Terri's face when she fell or feel my panic.

16

ATTACKS

Terri was involved in an incident involving another special needs adult that is almost too painful for me to talk about. No one told me this individual had been violent in the past. One day for some unknown reason she targeted my daughter, pulling a chunk of her hair out the size of a fist. Of course administration told me something like this would never happen again. They were to monitor Agnes more closely. In less than a week Agnes attacked Terri again. This time she strangled her leaving blue marks on her neck. It took three people to pull her off Terri. She was petrified of Agnes and so was I. I took her to the police station to document her injuries. I was furious.

I kept her at home for a long time while a solution to the problem could be determined. Once again administration guaranteed me Agnes would never attack my daughter again. A full-time shadow was placed with Agnes and they were to keep Terri and her in separate areas of the building. Because Terri missed her friends, I reluctantly allowed her to return.

One year later Agnes attacked Terri again attempting to strangle her as before. I went ballistic, refusing to listen to anything administration had to say. I found out the shadow had been removed from Agnes at the end of the year and I was enraged because no one told me. I no longer trusted them to protect my child.

Doc and I notified local politicians, the police, and wrote letters to state agencies including the Governor's office. Terri remained at home with us. We would not allow her anywhere near Agnes. Agnes was known to walk the streets of our small town. I was afraid we might run into her at the grocery store or the drugstore and she would try to attack Terri again. What would I do? How could I protect my child? We lived in fear.

In time we did allow Terri to return, but only on our terms. Agnes could no longer be at the same location with my daughter. We didn't allow Terri and Agnes to attend the same activities such as Special Olympics or bowling. Please understand we were not mad or upset with Agnes. We felt sorry for her, she was not as fortunate as Terri. She was not receiving proper medical care or the support of her family. Through the years Administration tried to convince us to allow Agnes back stating she was better; we never did. We were not taking any more chances with Terri's safety.

Terri and Amanda - Amanda's 35th birthday party, April, 2015

17

BEST FRIEND

Terri's best friend was Amanda. Amanda's mother, Linda, and I graduated from high school together. Linda knew I had a special needs child and I knew she had a special needs child, yet for some reason we had never introduced them to one another. In December 2014, I gave a wedding shower for my friends, Angela and Jeff. Linda and Amanda were on the invitation list. Our daughters clicked immediately.

After the wedding shower, Linda and I made it a point to get them together. We took them out to lunch or dinner. Sometimes we invited our husbands to tag along for dinner at Outback. Amanda and Terri sat side by side and held hands. They giggled and laughed as young girls do. Linda and I were as happy as the girls to see them having so much fun. Terri often told me in an earsplitting voice, "Momma, Amanda is my best friend." She had friends at the workshop she attended, yet her friendship with Amanda was different. She didn't see her every day as she did her other friends. So when we had plans that included Amanda, she could hardly wait for the day. It was all she talked about.

I have never known Terri to have as much fun as she had at

Amanda's 35th birthday party. She and Amanda danced to the sounds of The Temptations and The Drifters performed by a local DJ. They had so much fun. It did my heart good. I cried happy tears. Little did I know it was the last time I would cry happy tears.

The shared bond of special needs children has grown into a beautiful friendship for me and Linda. We often talk about wishing Terri and Amanda had had more time together. Their friendship only lasted a few months. They met in December 2014, and Terri died in May 2015. I continue to go out with Linda and Amanda. Terri would want me to spend time with her best friend. It hurts so badly to see Amanda sitting across the table from me and Terri is not there beside her. I work really hard at concealing my pain. I don't want to upset them.

Linda and I understand the heartbreak and joy of raising children with special needs. She has supported me in all of my endeavors to keep Terri's memory alive. I will forever be grateful to her.

Aunt Diane, Aunt Joyce, Momma and Terri, 2006

18

FAMILY

Terri held a special place in our family. We loved her through the good times and the bad and she loved us back tenfold. As my husband likes to say, I was her rock. She loved me with all of her heart and soul. She didn't like to be at home without me. When I was away, she would stand in the window in the laundry room and watch for me to come home.

Her grandmother held a special place in her heart as well. She came home from the workshop every day and called her grandmother. She never was one to carry on a long conversation on the phone. A typical phone call went like this, "Hello grandmother, this is Terri. I called to check on you. I have a new battery for my radio. I gotta go, bye." Her grandmother was never given the opportunity to speak.

She went with me to visit my mother's sisters, Aunt Esther and Aunt Hazel, in the nursing home. If I made the mistake of going without her on occasion, I was always reprimanded for leaving her behind. She was especially close to my daddy's sister, Aunt Molly. When she was older Aunt Molly went to live in an assisted care facility in Hamlet, North Carolina. Joyce and I went to visit her every three weeks and Terri went with us. En route there was a country store in Pageland, South Carolina that went all out for holidays with huge blown up characters for each holiday and a pumpkin patch in the fall. Joyce insisted we stop every holiday to take Terri's picture. Joyce didn't go anywhere without her camera. I am eternally grateful to her for taking hundreds of pictures of Terri through the years–each one a priceless memory for me now.

Out of the blue one day, Aunt Molly said to me, "Janice, you do know no one will ever take care of Terri the way you do." I was stunned. I decided then and there we would go to assisted care and room together when I was no longer able to take care of her. I never imagined she would leave me so soon.

Terri was at the center of every family reunion. There was a close bond between her and her second cousins. They enjoyed kidding around with her and she loved the attention. I have so many pictures of her having fun with her family. I cherish each and every one of them.

Terri looked forward to spending the night with her step-mom, Wanda, on Friday nights. She could hardly wait for Wanda to pick her up. As soon as she came in from the work-shop she started asking me to get her medicine ready. "Momma, Wanda will be here soon, get my medicine ready." She couldn't calm down until her medicine was in her pill box for the overnight sleepover.

Wanda's granddaughter, Haley, was usually there and she enjoyed playing with her. Haley was eight years old and Terri was 40, yet they considered themselves to be sisters. Wanda's nickname for Terri was "baby girl." She spoiled her by making her a huge breakfast every Saturday morning including liver mush, grits, eggs, and pancakes . . . the whole works. Liver mush is not on my list of foods to eat, yet it was a favorite of my daughter's. The weekend wasn't complete until they strolled through the local flea market. She held a special place in her heart for Wanda and Haley.

Terri suffered from anxiety and was always afraid something might happen to me. If she heard an ambulance, she would get upset, fearing the worse. "Something has happened to my Momma." Wanda would assure her I was okay. Considering Wanda as a backup mom comforted Terri.

If I was sick in bed, she hovered outside of my room imagining the worse when it was nothing more than the flu or vertigo. I tried to reassure her by telling her I was going to be fine, "Calm down, quit worrying, sweetheart."

Terri's daddy worked out of town and was seldom there on the weekends. It was always a special treat for her when he was able to make it home. She enjoyed their time together and came home bubbling with stories about her weekend with Daddy.

One picture of many Aunt Joyce took of Terri, Halloween, 2008

Terri with her daddy, 2000

Terri with her step-sister, Tessa, 2012

Terri and River, 2002

19

GRANDCHILDREN

Terri's stepsister and stepbrother both married and over time had children. We all thought Terri might be a little jealous of the grandchildren; however, that wasn't the case. She loved them and they loved their Aunt Terri. My husband and I have five beautiful grandchildren. Terri was age 30 when River was born, three years later Parker arrived, and within a few months the twins, Layla and Seneca, came on the scene. It was seven years later before the baby, Chucky, was born.

It didn't matter Terri was in her 30s and 40s when the grandchildren were young, she was one of them. She played with them like any other kid. Their favorite game was monster and of course, Terri was the monster. She would growl and chase them around the house. They ran shrieking and howling from room to room–finally ending in a heap of laughter. They played together on the Wii. Some of the games were a bit too complicated for Terri, but she held her own in the dancing game. The girls were in fierce competition with each other when it came to dancing.

Birthday parties for the grandkids were some of Terri's happiest times. A face painter was the featured event at one of the twin's birthday parties. She had her face painted just like the other children.

River was four or five years old before he realized Terri was not a child. One Sunday morning we were heading out the door to church when I heard this terrible ruckus. "What's going on with you two?"

River was noticeably upset, "Tell Terri she is not an adult. She is a kid just like me."

Terri was adamant, "I am too an adult."

They went back and forth for a while, so I stepped in to settle the argument, "River, even though Terri is an adult, she will always be a kid at heart and can play with you just like always."

I tried to help River understand, but it was hard for him to grasp Terri was an adult just like his daddy. No amount of explaining eased his mind.

When Parker was eight and nine years old she pretended to be Terri's teacher. She made out quizzes for Terri and read the questions to her. Terri didn't always get the answers right, but she gave it her best. Parker was bent on teaching Terri new things.

Until Chucky went to kindergarten he stayed with us while his mother taught school. Since the baby spent a lot of time at our house, Terri was very close to him. They ate breakfast together in the morning and played together in the afternoons when she came home from the workshop. At snack time she would share her apple with him and she was always careful not to wake him when he was taking a nap. Chucky was only two years old when Terri passed away.

One day shortly after she left us, I was lying across the bed crying. Chucky came in my room, crawled up on the bed with me and began talking about Terri. As young children do, he had all sorts of questions. "Mi Mi, why do you hold Terri's shirt when you take a nap? Why don't you go up to Heaven and bring her home? I want to play with her."

My feeble response, "I hold Terri's shirt because it comforts me. God wants her in Heaven with him. I can't go to Heaven and bring her home. I would if I could, sweetheart."

For a long time after she died he took her picture and placed it on the table in the den where he was playing with his Legos. It was his way of saying he missed her.

When Chucky was four years old we were riding home from church one Sunday morning and out of nowhere he said, "I have never held a baby."

I said, "You haven't? You will one day."

"Will it be a girl or a boy?"

"I don't know Chucky."

"What will I name the baby?"

"Can you think of some names?" I asked.

"I know I will name the baby Terri. Terri is a name for a girl or a boy."

He was sitting in his booster seat directly behind me. I was glad he couldn't see me because tears were streaming down my face. Even very young children grieve.

Chucky is six years old now. This past weekend we were coming home from Parker's volleyball tournament in Columbia. He began talking about Carolina and Clemson fans. His house is split–his father is a Clemson fan and his mother a Carolina fan. He is on the fence and trying to decide which way he wants to go. He asked me and my husband if we were Carolina or Clemson fans. Both my husband and I graduated from the University of South Carolina so you know where we stand. Then he asked about Terri, "Mimi, was Terri a Carolina or Clemson fan?"

"She was definitely a Carolina fan or she would not have been allowed to live in the house with us," Doc said jokingly.

It brought tears to my eyes to know Chucky hasn't forgotten her.

Recently Layla wrote a short story for school titled, *My Aunt Terri*. I couldn't stop crying when I read it. Layla is thirteen years old now, her insight and honesty is remarkable for someone her age. Following is an excerpt from her story:

"I remember one time asking Mimi why Terri didn't have a husband, because me being young I thought everyone had a husband or a wife. She said Terri wasn't going to get married, but something even cooler—Terri would live with her forever. Truly I still believe Terri is living with them. I think this because the house never felt empty when she left. Her presence is still there."

My grandchildren have been so blessed to have Terri in their lives.

Terri, 2014

20

HEAVEN BOUND

Angels came on Thursday, May 14, 2015 to take Terri home to be with Jesus. She was 43 years old. On the day before she had gone to the workshop like she did every day. We had an appointment with Mane Street Hair Designers to get our hair highlighted that afternoon. Terri was her usual happy self. She cut up with the girls and danced her last dance with Debbie.

After leaving the hair salon we met Doc at Applebee's for dinner. Terri was always excited about eating out and enjoyed her meal immensely. We came home; she took her nighttime medications and went to bed like any other night. Not long after going to bed, she came downstairs, "Momma, my stomach hurts!"

It's not unusual for a child to complain of a tummy ache, so I asked her if she wanted an Aleve. She took the Aleve and went back to bed. I didn't hear any more from her so I assumed she was fine.

Thursday morning I climbed the stairs like I did every morning to give her a bath. I would always wake her with, "Rise and Shine," but this morning would not be like any other. I found her face down on the pillow. I rushed to the bed and rolled her over. *She was gone.* My heart sank to my feet. Terror ripped through my body. I ran out to the balcony and started screaming for my husband. He and Chucky were outside feeding the cat. When he heard my screams, he came immediately sensing something was terribly wrong. I ran back to Terri's room. I can't explain why this detail is etched in my mind, but I still remember Doc standing there holding Chucky. He was wearing a hat. I see the exact color–it was camouflage green. I was screaming hysterically and told Doc to call Tessa to come get the baby. He ran downstairs, put Chucky in the play pen, called 911 and Tessa.

Doc and I placed Terri on the floor and began CPR. I thought the paramedics would never come. As they pulled into the driveway, I ran outside and begged them, "Please hurry! Please hurry! My baby isn't breathing." I still held some glimmer of unrealistic hope that Terri would wake up. Her eyes were listless, yet her skin was warm. When the paramedics came upstairs, I moved out of their way. I went in the adjoining room pacing the floor and begging God to save my baby.

When the paramedic shook his head no, I ran to Terri's side, kissing and caressing her face and hair, holding her hand in mine . . . knowing it was the last time I would feel her warm body next to mine. I vaguely recall the paramedics asking my husband for a list of Terri's medications. Thankfully Doc was there to handle those details; they were too much for my distraught mind. The coroner asked me at least five times if I wanted an autopsy performed. I repeatedly said, "No, I can't, it won't change the outcome." I couldn't bear the thought of my daughter's body being mutilated. Two police officers came to consult with the coroner. Of course, no foul play was determined.

Terri's doctor seems to think she had a heart attack, probably the result of the medications she took for so long. We will never know for certain why Terri died.

The house began to fill with people. I glanced out the window above where my daughter lie on the floor and saw neighbors lining the street and cars stopping in the road. Everyone was in shock. How could a perfectly healthy child die? I didn't leave Terri's side for what seemed like hours following her death. I was crying hysterically and pleading with God to help me. I remember saying over and over again, "Terri, I can't live without you, I can't!"

Doc nudged me in the back and said, "Please don't say that again, I need you."

When the funeral home came, my husband and Wayne lifted me off of the floor and carried me into another room. I couldn't be witness to my daughter leaving our home for the last time.

My preacher, Tim, was here immediately. I was trying to recall what had happened for him, but I was in such an intense state of shock–coherent thoughts were beyond my grasp. The funeral director, Evelyn, approached me while I was talking with Tim. I could not comprehend my daughter had just died; yet I was being asked to make decisions about the funeral service. *A funeral service? For my baby? No! No!* My mind cried. The only clear thought I had was to request a fresh arrangement of pink flowers to be placed on the mail box by the road. The usual silk arrangement of white flowers hung on the door of the home indicates someone has died. I couldn't accept my baby was gone.

Evelyn needed for me to decide on the day of the service because the funeral home was serving other families and she wanted to make certain I had the day of my choice. I decided on the following Sunday. I was stunned to hear myself say, "I want white balloons to be released at Terri's funeral." Having never seen this done before I can't explain why the idea occurred to me.

To make the next edition of our local newspaper the obituary had to written by 1 p.m. It was already 11 o'clock. Wayne wrote the most beautiful obituary. It captured Terri's true spirit. Tessa, Terri's stepsister, went in search of a picture for the obituary. Since Terri was not photogenic, Tessa had to hurriedly look through a huge collection of pictures to find a good one of her. It was an important picture and I wanted her to look her best. She cropped one taken at a recent cook-out for the obituary. Another hurdle in this nightmare had been taken care of.

My cousin, Carolyn, rushed over as soon as my sister called her. That day proved how much she loved me because she was not wearing any makeup. I have never known Carolyn to leave her home for any reason without makeup or her hair styled.

Throughout the day and night neighbors and friends came. I was numb all over and sat motionless and speechless while other people talked. I recall hearing them say, "I can't imagine what she is feeling." My granddaughters made cards that read, "Please don't be so sad, Mimi."

I wouldn't have made it through those first few days without Carolyn, Tessa, Wayne, and my sister, Diane. They were here around the clock to greet visitors, serve meals, make decisions . . . all the things I was incapable of doing. The days following Terri's death continue to be a blur. My only recollections of those days are me sitting in my rocking chair in a daze and crying–hoping someone would come to wake me from this nightmare.

The outpouring of love from our family, church family, friends, and community was overwhelming. Our neighbors gave me a statue of a little girl. I placed it in a natural area where I can see it from the kitchen window and be reminded of my precious daughter every day. Another friend, Shirley, gave me a beautiful necklace of angle wings. Cards with touching hand-written notes arrived daily by the dozens. I will always remember the love and support from my friends and neighbors.

21

THE FUNERAL SERVICE

Terri's funeral service was a true celebration of her life. There were so many beautiful flowers. Barbara, our friend from church, sent a flower with a headphone radio in it–another flower held pink watches. The church was filled with people who loved Terri (over 200 people attended). Her friends from the workshop were honorary pallbearers. Pastor Tim said he was honored to preside over her service, more so than any other service he had ever been a part of. He knew Terri well and spoke about the fun, loving, happy girl my daughter was. He even jested he could count on Terri to laugh at his jokes on Sunday mornings.

The pastor from Douglas Presbyterian Church, Harris Ricks, read *The Lint Child*. It brought tears to everyone's eyes. Doc's parents were long-time members of Douglas; we were often there for special occasions. Pastor Ricks told us Terri would always show him her watch after preaching. Smiling he said, "I wonder if she thought I preached too long."

Cameron, Terri's cousin and lifelong friend, gave a heart-warming eulogy. His words painted a picture of the extraordinary, unique person she was. He joked about Duracell, a battery plant, locating in our small town to keep their number one customer in batteries. He talked about growing up with her and the fun times they shared. Cameron was serious when he said we should all strive to live our lives as Terri . . . to laugh, to live with joy, and to love unconditionally.

The music chosen for Terri's service was beautiful. Our pianist, Nancy, played a wonderful arrangement of *Jesus Loves Me*. Mark Blackmon sang *I Bowed On My Knees and Cried Holy,* a song traditionally sung at services in my family for years. *How Great Thou Art* was a song chosen by Terri's paternal family. *You Are My Hero* was playing as we left the service. It is the perfect song to describe my feelings for Terri. She will always be my hero.

Each person was given a white balloon to release as they left the church. The bright blue sky filled with a host of white balloons floating toward heaven was a sight to behold.

The day of Terri's funeral was an unusually hot day. At the graveside Sue held an umbrella over me to protect me from the sun and brought a cooler of water for me or anyone who was thirsty. I was touched by her thoughtfulness. Since Sue is Tessa's mother-in-law, we feel more like family than friends. Together we share the same precious grandchildren.

At the graveside service, I did not cry. Sheltered by the shock, one face turned into another, their words sounding the same. It was an out of body experience. As if I was observing the service from a distance or in a dream.

Her marker reads, *There are no goodbyes for us, you will always remain in our hearts* and under her picture is the caption *Jesus Loves Me.*

Later that afternoon after the service Doc and I went to the park to see the flowers before they faded from the heat. We sat on a park bench at the side of Terri's grave until dusk. I recall saying to him, "Now the hard part begins."

He looked surprised, "What do you mean?"

I said, "Living without Terri."

God blessed me with the most wonderful daughter imaginable . . . so special and loving. She will live in my heart forever. I will cherish every moment we spent together on earth and will live every day for the rest of my life waiting to see her again in Heaven. It is my greatest honor to be her mother.

PART II

LIVING WITHOUT TERRI

1

LIFE WITHOUT TERRI

"Grief is the price we pay for love." – *Queen Elizabeth II*

Shock

Words do not exist to describe the shock I felt in the months following Terri's death. Suddenly without warning my life was shattered–forever changed. I lived in a daze and felt numb all over. I cried constantly and exhaustion was my ever-present companion. Incredible sadness overwhelmed me. My only relief from the excruciating pain was sleep.

I needed help to survive. The week after her death I was sitting in a grief counselor's office pouring out my heart and soul. The same week I made an appointment to see my general practitioner. He had been Terri's GP as well. He told me her death was a double whammy because our lives had been so intertwined. Caring for a special needs child for 43 years had required so much of my time and energy. Early mornings were spent giving her a bath and getting her ready for the day. Every decision was made around her schedule. Who would be waiting for her when she came home from the workshop at 2:30

every day? Who would take care of her if Doc and I made plans that couldn't include her? When she was well she went everywhere with me. A huge part of my life was suddenly missing. How would I ever fill the void? A part of me died the day she died.

My doctor was visibly shaken by Terri's death. He could see my pain and knew I couldn't make it on my own; I would need medical help to get me through. He prescribed an anti-anxiety medication to be taken as needed and at night for sleep. He promised me I would feel better in time–the pain would fade. Yet I couldn't imagine living my life without her. How could this happen to us? How? I became a member of a club I never wanted to join. Like other parents, I never allowed myself to think about the unimaginable and now here it was staring me in the face. I thought something like this happened to someone else, certainly not me. My innocence vanished. Now I live in fear someone else I love will be snatched away–my husband or one of my grandchildren. I constantly pray for God to keep my family safe and well.

Medication and cold face compresses were the only remedies for the panic attacks that plagued me for weeks after her death. Every day like a magnet I was drawn to the cemetery where she was laid to rest. I prayed desperately asking God to help me find my way in this world without her. I began a nightly ritual of watching the video shown at her funeral service and writing to her in a journal. Journaling has helped me to release some of the agonizing pain. Following is a journal entry I wrote not long after her death:

"*I try to imagine what it will be like to see you again when I get to Heaven. Will you be my same precious daughter? Will you be different from the way I remember you? Will you love me like you did here on earth? Will you put your head on my shoulder like you did so many times in church? Will you hold my hand and walk down the streets of gold with me? Will you take me to meet Jesus? I am so lost without you. God, please help me!"*

June 2015

It has been three years since her death and I continue the nightly ritual of watching her video and writing to her in my journal. I have learned rituals actually help with the healing process.

Denial

This can't be true! In the early days after she died I couldn't speak the word death. I thought if I didn't acknowledge it, it wouldn't be true. It was a reality my mind wouldn't allow me to accept. I didn't use past tense to describe Terri. Past tense would confirm her death. I refused to discuss the events surrounding her dying or anything that hinted at it. Everyone walked on eggshells around me, except precious two-year old Chucky. One day I was in the kitchen preparing the Sunday meal when Chucky asked me, "Mimi, do you miss Terri?"

I was caught off guard. I ran in the bedroom and fell apart. His sister, Parker, fussed at him for upsetting me. When I was able to get myself together, I came back to the kitchen and said to Chucky, "You didn't do anything wrong, sweetheart. Yes, I miss Terri very much and always will."

Guilt

The guilt I felt was unbelievable. I let my child down. She trusted me to take care of. I am her mother; I should have been able to protect her. Why? Why didn't I take her to the emergency room when she told me her stomach hurt? Maybe her life could have been saved. My grief counselor, Susan, tells me I feel this way because I want to change the outcome. If only I could!

A few weeks after her death, I was watching her video. This particular night there was a horrible thunderstorm brewing outside. The pain of guilt was so intense I went out on the back deck in the darkness. I was drenched and pulling at my clothes as I screamed and cried, "God, why did this happen to us?"

Lighting was all around me. It didn't matter if it struck me dead. I didn't deserve to live; I let my child down. Living without her was unbearable. I wasn't afraid to die. I wanted to be in Heaven with my baby.

Anger

Life isn't fair! I became very angry at God. One minute I was begging God to help me and the next minute I was shaking my fist toward Heaven and asking him Why? I never imagined God could be so cruel as to take my precious daughter away from me. We had been through so much together. Why did God allow this happen to us?

Shortly after we moved in to our new home, Joyce, Terri and I were browsing through a local print shop looking for Christmas presents. Terri fell in love with a picture of a guardian angel helping a small girl walk across a broken wooden bridge. It is an old print–one many of you have seen. As a child I remember it hanging in the living room of my grandmother's house. For Christmas that year I surprised Terri with the print. It hangs over her bed in her room. I haven't changed anything in Terri's room and never plan to. It is just as she left it. The guardian angel gave Terri a sense of security. She often said, "Momma my guardian angel watches over me while I sleep at night."

A few months after her death I went in her room hoping her things would bring me some minute form of comfort. I was in horrific pain. When I looked up at the print of the guardian angel, I went crazy–screaming over and over again at the angel, "How could you let my child die? She trusted you."

I believe God understands the pain of a parent who has lost their child and forgives us for questioning and becoming angry with Him. He understands our suffering and knows we are only human. Death was not a part of God's plan when he created us. Adam and Eve's sin in the Garden of Eden is why we suffer sickness and death. I actually believe God had a tear in his eye the day she died.

Lost Identity

I was totally preoccupied with her death. Joyce told me I had lost my identity when she died–so true. I was lost without her. I didn't know what to do with myself. She was no longer here for me to take care of. As my only child I would never hear her sweet voice calling me Momma again. My role as her mother and caregiver was gone.

My heart was broken and could never be mended. I felt so alone. I knew she was in Heaven, but that didn't relieve the pain. I needed her at home with me. My yearning for her was so intense, I prayed to die, "God, please don't leave me in this world to live without Terri."

Memory Wall. 2015

2

MEMORY WALL

"Those we love can never be more than a thought away ... for as long as there's a memory, they live in our hearts to stay."

— AUTHOR UNKNOWN

To occupy those lonely painful days I gathered every picture I could find of Terri. My friend, Karen, and I went shopping for the perfect picture album. We found one that held 600 pictures. The front cover reads, *"Love is patient, love is kind. It does not envy, it does not boast, it is not proud. It does not dishonor others, it is not self-seeking, it is not easily angered, it keeps no record of wrongs. Love does not delight in evil but rejoices with the truth. It always protects, always trusts, always hopes, always perseveres. Love never fails...."* I Corinthians 13: 4-8. If I have learned anything since her death, it is love never dies. I love her more today than I did when she was with me. I will love her until I take my last breath.

The idea of a memory wall occurred to me one day when I was on the Internet reading about the grief of losing a child. One mother said she had found comfort by creating a memory garden for her deceased son. I remembered seeing a picture of a wall filled with framed photos in various sizes in a magazine. They were displayed from wall to wall and ceiling to floor. The memory wall was born. Suddenly I had a purpose in life again–keeping Terri's memory alive.

I decided to place the memory wall outside of Terri's bedroom in the open balcony of our home. The photos would include her with all of her family members and friends. Since I didn't want it to be hodgepodge, I enlisted the help of a professional framer. Mark was so excited about the project, he could hardly contain himself. With Wayne's help, I chose the photos and the size of each one. To fill the wall we ended up with 47 framed photos and of those several are collages. Some are in color and some are black and white. For uniformity we chose solid black frames for all of them.

It seemed like forever, yet it was only a few weeks before Mark arrived to hang the framed photos. He is so talented; he arranged and hung them in a couple of hours. The wall is gorgeous and a true tribute to my daughter. Like so many things I ask myself, w*hy didn't I do this when Terri was with me?* It would have made her so very happy. We could have done it together.

I am proud of the wall, yet when I glance at it I am reminded that Terri is no longer at home with me. Quoting Barbara Streisand from the song *The Way We Were* the wall has become, "Misty water- colored memories of the way we were."

3

THE OUTDOOR SHELTER

For 22 years the workshop at our local Disabilities and Special Needs Board had been such an important part of Terri's life; I wanted to do something for her friends there in her memory. I mentioned the idea to my hair stylist and close friend Debbie. She was ecstatic about the opportunity to remember Terri in a special way and benefit her friends at the same time. Debbie is a natural born humanitarian and has organized a multitude of community fundraisers. She was the perfect person to lead this effort. I truly believe God puts angels on earth and Debbie is my Angel. I asked some of my friends to join the cause and The Terri Ledbetter Memorial Fundraiser Committee was formed. We are a group of thirteen ladies and as you will see we are a force to be reckoned with.

We met for the first time in July following Terri's death in May. There was so much energy in the room; ideas started flowing. Terri's stepmom, Wanda, suggested we build an outdoor handicapped accessible shelter at the workshop. The individuals are confined all day inside and can't go outside to enjoy God's beautiful creation. We decided to change that.

Since Terri loved music and never went anywhere without

her headphone radio, we wanted the benefit to revolve around music. A dance-a-thon would be perfect. This is how it worked. If you agreed to dance, you asked sponsors to donate $10/hour for each hour you danced. Terri was so loved it wasn't hard to find dancers. The event also included a silent auction, bake sale, face painting, balloon creations, and games for the children including bouncy houses. There was something to be enjoyed by everyone.

The benefit was held in the gym at North Elementary School on Saturday, October 24, 2015. It was a nice fall day and the turnout went beyond our expectations. At least 200 people came to enjoy the day.

Terri's friends danced to the tunes of the 80s and 90s. Our goal for the benefit was $10,000. We exceeded our wildest dreams and raised over $16,000. We were ecstatic. Surly we would have enough money to build the shelter.

The drafting instructor at our local vocational school was kind enough to draw the plans for us and we went in search for volunteers. It was easy to find volunteers for such a worthy project. However, we soon learned county zoning requirements would require a commercial contractor. Our first roadblock was finding a contactor willing to take on the liability for volunteers. Labor costs had not been a factor in our plans. We were a group of ladies with a cause, but no idea how to get there. We never dreamed the construction of the shelter would be such a monumental effort. We were certain of one thing; we were not going to give up.

I work for a local insurance company, Blackmon Insurance Group. One of the owners, Mark Blackmon, is a member of Kings Cause, a local gospel music group with a well-established following. Mark's group offered to help us raise additional funds. The committee met and agreed a concert by Kings Cause could help us cover the labor costs. The concert was scheduled for May 5, 2017, at Immanuel Baptist Church. It was a huge success. Terri's friends from the workshop were our special guests. They were in awe of the music. When the group sang, *I Bowed On My Knees and Cried Holy*, I was spellbound. This is the same song Mark sang at Terri's funeral service. Tears burned my eyes as I struggled to hold them back. Mark and three of his daughters sang *Jesus Loves Me* in memory of my daughter.

Since ticket sales alone would not bring in enough money to cover labor costs, Debbie had the brilliant idea of selling sponsorships for the program. Our goal for the concert was $10,000. We had a good turnout and met our goal. We were thrilled. Finally we had enough money to build the shelter. Or so we thought.

Chad Catledge with Perception Builders, a well-known commercial contractor, agreed to build the shelter. We would be required to pay for the materials and labor, his time would be free. The original shelter we had hoped to build was too costly. Jon Michael, also with Perception Builders, drafted new plans to fit our budget and finally we were on our way.

Yet another roadblock. Since the workshop is a state agency, the plans would need to be approved by the State. Additional requirements for a handicapped accessible shelter imposed on us by the State brought the total costs to over $32,000. We were short again. I was so depressed; I was tempted to give up. The committee had worked tirelessly for two years and our dream of an outdoor shelter in Terri's memory was still out of our reach.

Debbie saved the day. She recommended we ask local corporations for the additional funds. Armed with the scrapbook of the previous benefits I called on three corporations. In a week's time we had all of the money for the shelter. The last corporation I called on agreed to write a check for the remaining balance of over $3000. Our spirits soared.

Larry, a member of my church, called the morning after the

concert to say he could help us out with the picnic tables. Our church members were so generous; they donated all of the money and time needed to build the tables. Larry has told me over and over again how much he loved Terri and how special this project has been for him.

In April 2018, over two years after the first benefit, the committee met to plan the celebration of the shelter. We decided the big day would be Friday, May 18. It would be a drop-in from 11 until 3. We planned to serve hot dogs and homemade desserts. Terri's favorite music would be played and the decorations would include pink and white balloons.

Only one thing was missing–a memorial plaque. I called on Bob Doster, a local and well-known artist, to help me create the perfect plaque to memorialize my daughter. I was beside myself with excitement when I left his studio.

The memorial plaque is a true piece of art made of polished stainless steel and a line drawing of Terri wearing her headphones. It reads:

"Dedicated in loving memory of Terri Renee Ledbetter to her friends at the workshop. Terri attended the workshop for 22 years and left a handprint on the heart of every person she touched. Those who touch our hearts...stay in our hearts forever."

James, Bob's coworker, looked at every picture of Terri in the photo album of 600 pictures to get her smile just right for the line drawing. One of the people in attendance at the celebration said it looked as if she could start talking to us at any minute. The plaque is a marvelous tribute to my daughter. It is placed inside the fence at the shelter and is surrounded by a rock garden Doc and I made.

Shelter Celebration – Terri Ledbetter Memorial Fundraisers

*left to right, Donna Rogers, Carolyn Taylor, Denise Jordan, Wanda Ledbetter,
Janice Steele, Amanda Stegall, Carmen Evans, Shelia McWaters, Linda Stegall,
Earlene Horton, Debbie Crenshaw*

4

SHELTER CELEBRATION

The shelter celebration was awesome. It was a dreary rainy day, yet nearly 200 people came. Luckily we had enough tents to protect everyone from the rain. Michael Burgess with Burgess Funeral Home set up one of his 15x15 tents the day before. I had requested two tents, yet he only had one to spare. He was so concerned because he had only one tent; I overheard him telling Mark he would go to Wal-Mart and purchase additional tents. Several of my friends offered to bake cakes and cookies for the celebration. I tell you all this so you can understand how gracious the community has been to support this project.

Carrie, Terri's sister-in-law, was in charge of the music. She was streaming the music from her cell phone and much to our surprise the first song that played was Terri's favorite song, *Billie Jean*, by Michael Jackson. *It was as if Terri was there orchestrating the party.* A couple of her friends hit the floor dancing. To see them having so much fun filled my heart with joy and I knew all of our hard work was worth every minute of our time.

Several of the girls from the workshop came up to me and said in loud voices, "Terri was my best friend." One of my friends overheard one of the girls saying, "Terri was my best friend until she started hollering." As I mentioned in Part 1 she suffered from migraine headaches and would scream and cry for her mother when she was sick or upset.

The committee and their spouses worked so hard to make the celebration a success. Everyone had a job to do. I felt a little guilty because my only job was greeting everyone. I talked nonstop for three hours. I was moved by the amazement on everyone's faces when they saw the memorial plaque. Carrie couldn't stop crying. Tim, Terri's friend since high school, stood at the head of the plaque for the longest time. I could see his pain.

At the end of the celebration several of the committee members released 60 balloons. We didn't realize we were standing directly under a power line when we let them go. As we looked up we saw the balloons were floating toward the line. We were spellbound as they floated over and around the line. Not one balloon burst. I don't have an explanation except to say God or maybe even Terri's spirit was with us that day. I certainly could feel her all around me. I know how happy she was and how proud she was of her mother.

I held up really well for the celebration. I only had one melt-down. Before leaving I went inside the workshop to tell everyone goodbye. One of the men took my hands and was talking to me about Terri. I couldn't understand all he was saying, yet I knew he was telling me she was in Heaven and thank you for the shelter. He was so sincere and sweet. As I turned to leave I saw one of the girls wearing Terri's black and red Cinderella hoodie–one of many I donated to the girls at the workshop after her death. I was startled and gasped for breath. *Why wasn't Terri here to wear one of her favorite hoodies?* Debbie saw I was in trouble and grabbed my arm to steady me. Together we hurried out of the workshop so no one would see my tears. For the longest time we stood outside in the parking lot and Debbie listened as I told her how much it hurt. Debbie is a true friend.

The shelter celebration made the front page of our local newspaper. Mandy, a freelance writer, attended the celebration and wrote the article. She knew and loved both Terri and her grandmother. She was the perfect person to write the article and captured Terri's true spirit. She titled it *A Tribute to a Joyous Soul*. At church the following Sunday morning several people commented on how much they enjoyed reading the article. It is a true love story. A story about the love of a mother and a loving community dedicated to seeing the project through in spite of all of its roadblocks.

5

FINDING MY WAY

"God has a perfect plan for your life."

— LAILAH GIFTY AKITA, PEARLS OF WISDOM: GREAT MIND

I desperately needed to occupy my mind and fill my empty days. I prayed constantly for God to help me find my way in this world without my child. Before Terri's death, Mark and Scott Blackmon, brothers and owners of Blackmon Insurance Group, had asked me to join their agency. Years earlier we had worked together as agents for a local insurance company. I passed on the opportunity at the time because I was working as an adjunct instructor for a local community college and I had Terri to take care of. The summer after her death they approached me once again. Open enrollment was coming up in October and it is a busy time for insurance agents. They asked if I would be willing to answer the phone, make appointments, file, and greet clients. I felt this was God's answer to my prayers. I needed to stay busy so this time I accepted their offer and began working for them in October, five months after Terri's death.

It has been a win-win situation for both parties. I have

helped them grow their business and they have helped me survive the loss of my child. Since Terri has not been in my office environment, I go there for respite. At home I am constantly reminded of her, I see her everywhere I turn. I see her sitting at the foot of my rocking chair when I take a coffee break. I see her leaving in the morning to board the van for the workshop and coming through the door in the afternoon. I see her sitting in the dinette chair watching me cook Sunday dinner. Parents who have lost a child are familiar with the empty chair. But for me an empty window really brings home my loss. I see her standing at the laundry room window every day watching for me to come home from work. My eyes are drawn to that window every time I drive up the driveway. I can see her as clearly as if she were standing there. Coming home will never be the same for me.

To cope with losing Terri I found it necessary to compart-mentalize my grief. In other words, leave it at home when I go to work and pick it back up when I come home in the evening. Consumed with my work I am a different person on the job. Once I come home the agonizing pain overwhelms me once again. This strategy works for the most part, yet there are times when a client asks me how I am doing and the tears flow as I tell them how hard it is to live without Terri. The other day her van driver came in the office. She loved Terri so much. As I listened to her talk about Terri the pain washed over me like a tsunami and I was swallowed up with grief. I had to come home and go to bed. Sleep is still my only real relief from the unbearable pain of losing my precious daughter.

On another day not long after Terri left me, a client was making small talk and asked if I had children. All parents who have lost children face this question sooner or later–it comes out of nowhere leaving you blindsided. I struggled to catch my breath. I hadn't thought about how I would respond to that question. Should I say I have a step-daughter and step-son and leave it at that? Should I say I have a daughter in Heaven? I cried as I told the lady my daughter had recently passed away. I felt sorry for her, she was so apologetic. She never meant to upset me.

We never know when an unintentional comment or a memory will catch us off guard. There really is no way to prepare for it.

*July 2019 Meeting, an old-fashioned July 4th cookout
with balloons released to our children in Heaven*

6

A NEW ROAD

"Grief knits two hearts in closer bonds than happiness ever can; and common sufferings are far stronger links than common joys."

— *ALPHONSE DE LAMARTIN (1790-1869)*

My sister had taken Doc and me to a Compassionate Friends Support Group meeting in Charlotte the week after Terri's death. It is a worldwide support group for the families of a deceased child. The group had a balloon release at this meeting. I wrote a note to Terri and attached it to the balloon. It read:

"Terri, my precious daughter, I love you with every ounce of my being. My world is shattered and my heart is broken. I don't know how I will live without you. God blessed me with the most wonderful daughter imaginable, so special and loving; you will live in my heart forever. I cherish every moment we spent together here on earth. Thank you for loving me with the most amazing love. Love forever, Momma."

Hundreds of balloons floating toward Heaven on a bright sunny afternoon were breathtaking. While this part of the meeting really touched me, I wasn't prepared to answer questions about my daughter's death. I was in a deep state of shock and didn't want to believe it had actually happened. I kept thinking I was going to wake up from this awful nightmare. I decided it was too soon for me to be in a support group. I felt safer in private sessions with my grief counselor.

My husband was trying, yet he couldn't understand what I was going through. He loved Terri and was grieving too, but as a stepfather his grief looked a lot different than mine. And that's okay. Everyone grieves differently. My sister, Diane, who had also lost her only son 12 years earlier, tried to prepare him on what to expect from me as I grieved the death of my child. Yet he wasn't able to grasp the depth of my grief. It seemed as if no one understood my sorrow. I felt so alone and isolated in my walk with grief.

Before Christmas in 2016, it occurred to me other parents were suffering just like me. It had been a year and half since Terri's death and the timing for a support group seemed right to me. I needed to bond with other people who had experienced child loss. I told my husband I wanted to start a support group for parents who had experienced the death of a child in my hometown.

In January of 2017, I met with my preacher about the idea of starting the group. He felt it would be a great outreach program for our community. He suggested we meet in the church office building. In February we held our first meeting. With the help of a close friend, Denise, I put together a flyer and named the group A New Road. I made a list of all the people in our small town who had lost a child and called to invite them to our first meeting. I also ran an announcement in the local newspaper.

Including my preacher, 11 people attended our first meeting. My sister, Diane, drove three hours to come home and support me. Pastor Tim opened with a prayer. Diane read an article related to child loss and some people in the group shared their heartbreaking stories. The meeting went well and it was the beginning of lifelong friendships.

We continue to meet the first Tuesday of every month. It is an open meeting, meaning parents can join us at any time. I can't tell you how much the group has helped me. To be on the same journey with other people who have experienced child loss gives me hope. I no longer feel so alone.

The support group meetings have strengthened mine and Doc's marriage. He couldn't understand my grief until he attended the meetings. After hearing other people talk about their grief he has come to the conclusion that I am not going crazy after all. Attending the meetings together has given us the opportunity to share our feelings. I don't tell him often enough how much I appreciate his support. The group has been an answer to prayer. God knew my grief for Terri was placing a strain on my marriage and I needed friends who I could bond with.

Christmas of 2017 our group planned a Candle Lighting Service for parents and their families. The service was held in the sanctuary at Immanuel Baptist Church. Formal invitations were printed and sent to people in our community who had lost a child. Brochures about the service were distributed to local churches, funeral homes, and hospice houses.

Debbie, a faithful member of our group and a wonderful floral designer, decorated the church and the social hall. It was breathtaking. The ambiance for this touching service was created with white hydrangea and white candles to signify the dignity and respect we felt for our deceased children. The altar and pulpit were lined with eight bronze obelisk candle towers, each holding 12 candles. A large all-white flower arrangement surrounded by numerous white candles of varying shapes and sizes decorated the altar table.

The service was both heart wrenching and uplifting with wonderful music, prayer, scripture readings, and the touching message by Pastor Easler of Corinth Baptist Church in Gaffney, South Carolina, who had lost his six-year old son in a train accident at an amusement park six years earlier. The Pastor's heartfelt words and prayer for encouragement amidst the lovely candle-lit sanctuary created a wonderful opportunity for us to honor our deceased children and to move forward and celebrate the Christmas season.

Following the service a reception was held in the social hall. The mood of the social hall reflected the sanctuary. The memory table was adorned with a tall lantern to allow the white candle to burn above the pictures of our departed children.

Sixty to seventy people came to remember their deceased child at the Christmas season in a very special way. Some of the people who came had lost their child recently, for others it had been one or two years, or twelve, twenty, or even longer since their child had died. The age of the child or parent is not a factor when the child dies. The grief for the parent is the same regardless of age.

It is not easy to live with the loss of a child and the holidays are especially difficult. To be in the company of people bonded together by the love of a deceased child and the mutual understanding of one another's pain was an awesome and heartwarming experience.

Several of our members wrote testimonials in the brochure for the service about how much the support group has helped them.

"Scripture says we should support one another. Our support group has been a lifeline for me during the past year. We all understand the pain of losing a child. However, we are not alone on our journey. We have each other and Jesus has promised not to leave us or forsake us."
Terry Robinson

.   .   .

"TALKING about the death of my son can be difficult. But also it is an important way I cope with the loss. The group has helped me deepen my understanding of grief and bereavement." Adam Biggs

"THE LOSS of my precious daughter is a loss like no other. A New Road has given me strength, courage, and hope for tomorrow. I no longer walk this road of unimaginable grief alone." Janice Steele

FOLLOWING IS a poem read at Terri's Funeral Service and also printed in the program for the Candle Lighting Service:

God's Lent Child
By Edgar Allen Guest

I will lend you for a little while, a child of mine, He said.
For you to love the while she lives, and mourn for her when
she's dead.
It may be six or seven years, or twenty-two or three.
But will you, till I call her back, take care of her for Me?
She'll bring her charms to gladden you, and should her stay be
brief,
You'll have her lovely memories, as solace for your grief.
I cannot promise she will stay, since all from earth return,
But there are lessons taught down there, I want this child to
learn.
I've looked the wide world over, in search for teachers true.
And from the throngs that crowd life's lanes, I have selected you.
Now will you give her all your love, or think the labor vain.

Nor hate me when I come to take her home again.
I fancied that I heard them say, 'Dear Lord, Thy will be done!'
For all the joys Thy child shall bring, the risk of grief we'll run.
We'll shelter her with tenderness, we'll love her while we may.
And for the happiness we've known, forever grateful stay.
But should the angels call for her, much sooner than we
planned.
We'll brave the bitter grief that comes, and try to understand.

THIS POEM SPEAKS volumes to every parent who has had to give their child back. I can't recall if I heard this poem before Terri's death. If I had, it took on an entirely different meaning for me when it was read at her service. Amanda's mother, Linda, framed it for me. It hangs in Terri's room. Sometimes at night when the house is quiet I go up to her room to reflect on its words.

The Candle Lighting Service has become an annual event for our support group. This past year's service (2018) was the most meaningful service I have ever been a part of. I didn't think it was possible, yet the sanctuary was grander than last year. The Christmas decorations combined with Debbie's candle lighting decorations created a sense of wonder. The altar table was adorned with 30 or 40 white candles in varying heights burning brightly and surrounded with magnolia leaves. The steps leading up to the pulpit were flanked on each side with three candle-lit candelabras–each one held 12 candles. Tall white candles burned in each of the ten stained-glassed windows. The glow of all of those candles was magnificent. As you entered the sanctuary you knew this would be a truly special time. Strangers bonded together by the death of a child talked and hugged each other.

Rather than a guest speaker, the planning committee

decided on a musical service with scripture readings so we could devote the major part of the service to lighting candles in quiet remembrance of our children who are no longer with us, but will never be forgotten. The music was awe-inspiring. As guests were seated, David Faulkenberry and his wife Katy, a guitar and French horn duet, played several selections. The service opened with the dynamic performance by Jerry Hollis. Eyes filled with tears as he sang *I Bowed On My Knees and Cried Holy*. The serene mood continued as scripture readings were interspersed with four short songs sung by the congregation, led by song leader Debra Rowell.

The lights were dimmed and Shelly Boulder led the candle lighting part of the service. Dressed in a white robe she began with a brief humbling message of encouragement and hope for the congregation. The candles were lit by passing the flame along the rows of pews, from one person to the next. This year we named the child we were remembering as we lit the candle. My candle was the first one lit so I set the tone for this part of the service. Doc was a candle lighter. As he lit my candle I simply said, "I light this candle in memory of my daughter, Terri Ledbetter." The church was quiet and reverent as the flame was passed from person to person. Each name was clearly heard as it was called. Choir bells hummed in the background as each candle was lit.

After the candles were extinguished Debbie Jaillette played an amazing arrangement of *Jesus Loves Me* on the piano. The service closed with the heartwarming poem *We Remember Them* from Gates of Prayer, Judaism Prayerbook read by Debbie Dunn.

A reception followed in the church social hall. A fresh white floral arrangement of lilies with a tall angel and burning white candle was the focal point of the memorial table where we displayed pictures of our children.

This year our invitation list included family and friends–

over one hundred people attended. The church was filled with people on every pew. We received so many compliments on how touching the service was and how much it meant to be able to remember our children in such a special way at Christmas. For me the service to remember Terri with family and friends helps me as I move forward with the season. Since I have set aside time just for her it is not as hard for me when the family gathers for Christmas.

If you are grieving the loss of a child, I hope you will consider a support group in your area. Compassionate Friends offers over 600 meeting places around the country. Google Compassionate Friends to find a location near you. Or you may want to consult your local newspaper to find a small support group in your community like our group.

Feel free to join our group at www.hopeforgrievingparents. com. It will provide you with much needed emotional support as you walk your path of grief. Grab this lifeline!

COMPLICATED GRIEF

"There is sacredness in tears. They are not the mark of weakness, but of power. They speak more eloquently than ten thousand tongues. They are messengers of overwhelming grief ... and unspeakable love."

— *WASHINGTON IRVING*

Complicated grief is described as grief that does not go away. A person remains in the acute stages of grief long after the loss of a loved one–one year, two, five or longer. Some psychologists refer to it as being stuck. I have been told by two professionals I suffer from complicated grief. I first heard the term when a hospice nurse who was treating my twin sister told me it was clear to her I was suffering from this condition. I assumed complicated grief was a term contributed to multiple deaths occurring in one's life over a short period of time. My daughter had suddenly passed away and now only six months later I was losing my twin sister–my lifelong friend and biggest supporter.

Joyce tried so hard to understand what I was going through when Terri died. As sick as she was, she was there for me. Every day I would leave work, go by the park where Terri is buried and on to Joyce's to spend time with her. I was in such despair over losing Terri I couldn't grasp the reality that my sister was dying. I kept thinking she had more time. Terri died in May and Joyce died in December of the same year. My grief for Joyce has in some way been overshadowed by my grief for Terri.

My grief counselor agrees with the hospice nurse. I suffer from complicated grief. In an attempt to understand the condition I read the book, *The Other Side of Complicated Grief,* written by Rhonda O'Neill. If you think you may be suffering from the condition, you may want to read this book. Similar to my situation, Rhonda lost her husband in a plane crash and two years later lost her son to kidney failure. In her book she talks about the alchemy of grief:

"A part of the healing process is getting to a point where you can recognize how blessed you were to have experienced such a life-changing love. That is when your memories will become treasures. Treasures that are always yours and can never be lost. You will always be connected to your loved one."

Monday, May 14, 2018 has been three years since my daughter went to Heaven. I haven't reached the other side of complicated grief; yet, I am better. I don't cry as often or as long. I have more moments of happiness than I did soon after Terri's death. I can connect with my grandchildren and truly enjoy the time we spend together without feeling guilty. My grief counselor told me in my early days of grief I would never be as happy as before, yet there would be moments of happiness. She also told me I would always and forever miss Terri. She was right. I miss everything about her. I miss her beautiful face, her presence, her laughter, and most of all her love. I think about her constantly. My grief runs right under the surface, it is always with me.

8

HAPPENINGS

Shortly after Terri passed away I had the most wonderful dream. Terri, Doc, and I were walking somewhere–I don't know where. Terri was in the middle and we were all holding hands. Terri was walking a step in front of us as if she were leading us. I remember the look on her face vividly and always will. She had the happiest look, almost angelic. We were all three smiling. Doc said it was a sign from God we would all be together again one day.

I am not sure if this was a vision or a dream–I thought I was awake. One morning I was lying in bed thinking about getting up. Suddenly Terri was sitting beside me–so close I could have touched her. She was wearing a white shirt and holding her headphone radio in her lap. Being so near to her was a feeling I can't explain. I didn't want to get up because I knew she would go away. I stayed there for the longest time basking in her presence.

Shortly before Terri's grandmother passed away I had a vision of a bright light in my bedroom window. I had just gone to bed when a shimmering bright light appeared in the window. It was so bright it was almost blinding. It covered the entire window. My first thought was something had gone wrong with my eyes. I sat up in the bed and looked around the room. Everywhere in the room everything was as it should be. I was blinking and looking at the light trying to make sense of it. I wasn't afraid. I was in awe of the bright light. Was it the Holy Spirit? Was it Terri's spirit? The bright light stayed in the window for several minutes. I was so spellbound I didn't think to wake Doc to ask him if he could see it.

The light in the window appeared a second time. It was the night after the Candle Lighting Service in 2018. I was on such a high from the exhilarating service we had experienced earlier in the day, I was unable to sleep. This time the light would fade, come back and fade again. I just knew it was Terri communicating with me the only way she could–letting me know how much she loves me and sharing my excitement for the service.

This time I woke Doc up to see if he could see it. If you knew my husband you would know he does not like to be awakened from a deep sleep. He glanced at the window but the light had already faded; he growled about being woken up and went back to sleep. I continued to stare at the light until I finally fell asleep from exhaustion. Now at night when I go to bed I lie there hoping the light will appear again. It gives me much comfort.

This past summer at the beach I was standing out on the balcony and the only star in the sky appeared to start dancing every time I looked at it. I called Doc out on the balcony and he agreed with me–the star was dancing. I returned to the balcony several times during the night and each time the star would dance. I was mesmerized. Was it Terri communicating with me from Heaven?

A close friend, Jimmie, had given Terri a solar powered flower before she passed away. It sits in the kitchen window. Whenever I look at it, it starts dancing. One day it was dancing wide open. Terri must have been really excited that day. I don't have an explanation for these happenings. I only know they make me feel Terri is near to me.

I pray nightly for God to send me a dream about Terri and the ability to remember it in the morning. I need to be close to her, to feel her presence. Some mornings when I awake I know I have been dreaming about her, yet I can't recall the dream. It is so frustrating. I thought I was the only person who prayed for dreams about their child, but when I mentioned it in a support group meeting, other members were nodding their heads in agreement. They pray the same prayer. It is sad when the only way you can spend time with your child is in a dream.

Terri with Santa Claus, 2012

9

HOW I SURVIVE DIFFICULT TIMES

Blessed are those who mourn, for they will be comforted.
Matthew 5:4

All holidays present difficult challenges for the parents grieving the loss of their child. The two most difficult days for the parent are the child's birthday and the date of their child's death. Terri's birthday is especially difficult for me because it was her favorite day. She talked about her birthday all year long—starting the very next day after it, telling everyone she came in contact with she had a birthday coming—December 16.

We continue to celebrate her birthday just as we did when she was with us. A small group of family and close friends dine at one of Terri's favorite restaurants. To honor her on the first birthday after her death, we chose Angels from a local Angel Tree. Rather than buying Terri birthday presents we bought Christmas presents for children who would not have presents under their tree without our help. The second birthday, I framed a picture of Terri sitting on Santa Claus' lap for everyone. This past birthday, I bought a memory book and everyone recorded their favorite memory of Terri. The book is so special to me, I treasure it. The front cover reads, "Love never fails, 1 Corinthians 13:8." Following are a few of the memories:

Debbie Crenshaw wrote, *"Terri showed us how to love, laugh, and live. She will always be in my heart."*

Terri's cousin, Merridy wrote, *"Growing up with Terri taught me to enjoy the simple moments of life. She was so excited to share her happy moments with others. She shared her joy of music with such excitement. No one loved Michael Jackson like Terri . . . ."*

Her stepbrother, Scott, wrote, *"I remember well how sweet and innocent you were. That is something I will never forget. Even days when I wasn't feeling like talking or being social you would make me smile. I know Christmas and your birthday were your favorite times of the year. Sometimes that would be all you talked about. I will also never forget how much you loved music. From the time we were kids it was the one thing you never gave up. The swing and bicycle you grew out of, but your radio and headphones never left your side. I love you Terri and still miss you."*

Our friend, Angela, wrote, *". . . . I can just see her sweet and innocent face—always so happy and never met a stranger. We were all so blessed to know her."*

Her sister-in-law, Carrie, wrote, *". . . . my favorite thing about her, what I treasure the most was her joy to connect with people—to talk with others whether she knew them or not. She did this with such excitement for life and sharing it with others. It was special and so was she . . . ."*

Her Aunt Diana wrote, *"My little Terri-bug—talking about her birthday all year round. She would say to me, 'I'm your little girl, ain't I Aunt Diana?' – and she was indeed."*

Her Aunt Diane wrote, *"I will always remember your smiling face and how you always met me at the door and told me 'Aunt Diane, I am so happy you are here.' But most of all I remember how you came up to my room and said, 'Aunt Diane, I love you and I love my* momma. Aunt Diane, you know I love my momma.' You made sure I knew you loved your momma."

Her niece, Layla wrote, *"I remember when me and Terri would run through the house and play monster, or she would let us listen to her Walkman, or how we would always get a Terri hug from her when she came home from the workshop. I really miss her and think about her every day."*

I can't put up a Christmas tree; it continues to be too painful. On Christmas Eve for 43 years I placed Terri's presents under the tree. She knew Santa Claus didn't really exist, yet we loved to pretend he did. Like other children she was anxious for the Elf on the Shelf to appear every year to make certain she was a good girl.

For the first couple of years after her death, I was unable to have family over for Christmas as in years past. I know I am getting better because this past Christmas after three years I resumed some family traditions. I decorated the mantel since I would not be decorating a tree. Doc and I hosted the Burch Christmas Reunion (my mother's family) as we had done so many times before. We cooked dinner for our immediate family. The grandkids hardly noticed there was not a Christmas tree. We piled the presents on and around the coffee table in the den. I surprised myself at how well I did. I have learned to always have a plan for difficult days; I force myself to do the difficult things, it is not nearly as hard as I anticipated it would be.

As I write this book, May 13, 2018, it is Mother's Day, another sad day for a parent who has lost their child. Terri was always giddy with excitement when she gave me my Mother's Day card. Doc helped her select the card and she signed it. I read it to her and told her how blessed I was to be her mother and how much I loved her. She said in her sweet, innocent voice, "Momma, I love you"–three simple words that melted my heart.

Even after three years, I have so many family members and

friends who continue to remember me and my loss on Mother's Day. Sue texted me this message today, "Janice, I want you to have a happy Mother's Day . . . I know you think it is impossible . . . but you deserve a restful, happy day because you are the BEST, KINDNEST, MOST LOVING MOTHER . . . EVER. Terri wants you to be happy, because you made her so very happy." Jeff texted me to say, "Just wanted to say love u." And Carrie wanted Doc and me to know she was thinking about us today. My husband lost his mother this past year so we both are grieving. Terry, a fellow member of A New Road support group, sent me the most beautiful card this past week. The love and support from my family and friends continues to amaze me. God has truly blessed me.

Today, my sister Diane and I decided to drown out the sorrow of Mother's Day by going shopping. My sister lost her only son 13 years ago to cancer at age 39. At difficult times a diversion from the awful pain is the only way to survive the day. We met at Chico's. She is an expert at putting the right outfits together including accessories. She has been and continues to be a great source of support for me in my walk with grief. She has been where I am and can truly relate to what I am going through.

Terri's date of death, May 14, is an awful day for me. For weeks before this date, I am depressed and dread the thought of living through another anniversary day. Doc and I have made it a tradition to go to the beach for a sabbatical from the grief. I can't bear the thought of staying at home and reliving that awful morning . . . the worst day of my life.

It makes me incredibly sad to go to church without Terri. When she first died I truly didn't think I would ever be able to go back. How could I go to church without my daughter by my side? Terri sat beside me in Sunday school and preaching. She put her head on my shoulder and sometimes we held hands. Those are some of my happiest memories.

A friend of mine suggested I change things up a bit to help me cope. I go in a different door and sit in a different place for Sunday school and preaching. It is still one of the hardest things I have to do, but I force myself to get out of bed and dress for church every Sunday.

Nowadays I sit in church and imagine her head on my shoulder. It brings tears to my eyes. Yes, I still cry in church. Just sitting there thinking about her and wishing she were with me is more than I can bear.

Not long after Terri died one of my friends, Frances, suggested I sleep with one of her shirts. She said it would give me something to hold on to. I asked my husband to go upstairs and bring down the shirt Terri wore the day before she died. I continue to sleep with it every night though I can no longer smell her scent. I even take it on vacation with me. I hold it close to my heart as I sleep. When I roll over during the night I make certain her shirt goes with me. I snuggle with it when I take naps. Holding something of Terri's helps me feel close to her.

I sit in my rocking chair with a cup of coffee and spend time thinking about Terri every evening when I come home from work. I have a picture of her on the table beside my chair. I talk to her while I am sitting there. My grief counselor assures me this is not unusual for a grieving parent. She says anything that helps is acceptable. I kiss her picture and tell her goodnight every night before I go to bed. Her picture goes with me on vacations.

My daddy left us girls a hand-written note. It reads, "Think of all the good times we have had, remember the happy times." Whenever my mind wonders off on the struggles Terri and I shared, I try to change my train of thoughts to the legacy of love my daddy left us–the good times.

10

NIGHT TO SHINE

A local church, Unity Associate Reformed Presbyterian Church, was chosen to host Night to Shine, sponsored by the Tim Tebow Foundation on February 8, 2019. It is a special night for school age children 16 and over and adult individuals with special needs in our community to experience an unforgettable prom dance.

My friend, Debbie, attends Unity ARP Church and served on the Night to Shine Committee. She has organized many local community events, yet I have never known her to be as excited as she was about this particular event. She asked me to help her solicit donations. We couldn't have built the shelter without Debbie and I was grateful for the opportunity to return the favor. It was especially meaningful for me because it included Terri's friends. Terri wouldn't be there, yet I was determined to help her friends have the time of their lives.

Debbie asked me to be a buddy. A buddy spends the evening with a special needs guest while the parents or caregivers enjoy the Oasis Room–an evening of total relaxation.

At first I told Debbie I would not be strong enough to be a buddy. Knowing Terri wouldn't be there was too much for me. I was afraid of breaking down and spoiling the night for the other prom goers. After praying about it and asking God to give me the strength I said, "Yes, if I can be Amanda's (Terri's best friend) buddy." Terri would be happy to know I was spending the evening with her best friend.

Amanda's mother bought her a gorgeous red dress and a faux fur stole for the occasion. She wore a sequined black hat. Similar to Terri and her radio Amanda has a thing for hats. She wears a hat everywhere she goes. Of course, Amanda's mother, Linda, and I thought she was the most beautiful girl there. Amanda was over the top with excitement anticipating the big night.

February 8 finally rolled around on the calendar. I met Amanda's parents at admissions. They kissed Amanda as they left for the Oasis Room and we boarded the limousine for the social hall. We were greeted by a paparazzi of volunteers and the announcement of our arrival by a local news station as we exited the limousine to walk the red carpet. Cameras were flashing everywhere.

We danced the entire evening stopping only long enough to visit the hair and makeup station, pose for a professional photo shoot, and eat our catered meals. Amanda and I had the time of our lives. She was full of laughter as we joined the soul train and held hands and danced in a circle with other party goers.

The finale of the evening was the crowning of each of our special guests as kings and queens complete with a balloon drop. Amanda didn't want to give up her hat so her mother and I placed her tiara over it. Her parents had joined us for the big moment of the night.

It was an awesome experience for me–watching Amanda and Terri's other friends having so much fun. I cherish every memory from that night. God answered my prayers. I didn't break down until I arrived home. I surrendered my pent up emotions and cried for hours before falling asleep exhausted from the grief of losing my child.

Linda bought the video from the Night to Shine. This past Saturday our families enjoyed movie night. We met for dinner and came back home to watch it. Amanda was excited to know she was on TV. Terri would have been too.

11

A LIFETIME OF GRIEF

"The reality is you will grieve forever...you will learn to live with it. You will heal and rebuild yourself around the loss you have suffered. You will be whole again, but you will never be the same. Nor should you be the same, nor should you want to."

— ELIZABETH KUBLER-ROSS

The other night my grief counselor told me grief will always be a part of my life. Time doesn't heal the grief of losing a child. Grieving is the way I stay in touch with Terri. I have no intentions of ever letting her go. She will always be a part of my life. Some people have said to me I need closure. There is no such thing as closure when you lose a child.

There is no way for me to gloss over child loss. It is an emptiness I can't explain. Not just once in a while, but every night when I go to bed I am acutely aware Terri is not in her bed–her room is empty. Every morning I wake up to the realization I am facing another day without my precious daughter in my life. I can't tuck my child in bed at night or wake her in the morning with "Rise and Shine."

Sometimes when I am at home alone I sit in my rocking chair and scream Terri's name as loud as I can. As if my voice could somehow reach up to Heaven and bring her home to me. The parent who has lost a child never "gets over it." We will grieve until we take our last breath. Yes, we learn to live with the excruciating pain because we do not have a choice. We would give anything to have our child here with us and our life back to normal again; but, of course, this is not reality.

If you have not lost a child it is impossible for you to comprehend our suffering. You wonder why we continue to grieve when sometimes it has been years since our loss. Those of us who have joined the club of child loss are glad you don't understand. We would never want you to experience the agony of losing a child. I have learned to overlook the blank stares when I mention my daughter's name or talk about watching her video or writing to her every night in my journal. Please understand, we love our deceased children just as much as you love your living children. We talk about our children because we constantly think about them and more than anything in the world we want to keep their memory alive. The most compassionate act of kindness you can offer bereaved parents is simply listening as they talk about their child.

Today at work I overheard two people talking about their children going off to college and how difficult it is for them. I wanted to scream, "Your children are coming home on weekends and holidays, my child is never coming home again." Of course, I said nothing. I didn't understand when I was on the other side of the fence either.

Even now Terri's death seems surreal to me. It is hard for me to realize it really happened. What did I do to deserve this? Every day is a challenge when you are living without your child. I can't enjoy the simple things in life as I did when she was with me. When I look at the beautiful blue sky on a bright sunny day, it is not as bright as it was when Terri was here.

In every day conversation I find myself saying before Terri died or since Terri died. My life will forever be divided into two parts . . . before or after she died. My life is irrevocably changed. I don't see the same person looking back at me when I look in the mirror. This new person looking back is sad.

My counselor tells me I am learning to live with the pain in one hand and enjoy life again in the other hand. She is right. I do have hope for tomorrow. I look forward to those happy moments I share with my family and friends . . . especially my grandchildren. They are my saving grace.

When Terri died I lost interest in most things. On the good days I find myself slowly resuming some of my previous activities. For the first time since she left me I am working in my yard again. Before Terri died I had groundcover white roses planted on both sides of the driveway. In the spring of the year the roses were gorgeous. I was constantly getting compliments on them. They were in full bloom when Terri died in the month of May. Each year as the summer progressed, the roses would need constant pruning to keep them from growing out over the driveway. For this reason my husband despised them, so shortly after Terri's death and when I was at my weakest moment, he dug them up. I was in too much despair to protest. Since Terri would not be here to see them bloom again; I didn't care they were gone. I couldn't bear the thought of seeing them in bloom when spring returned.

This past weekend I replaced them with pink drift roses in Terri's memory. Drift roses will not grow as big as groundcover roses. I wrote to her in my journal about them:

Terri,

It has been a good day. Doc and I planted pink drift roses in your memory where the white roses bloomed when you were with us.

Looking at bare places on each side of the driveway when I came home every day was just another reminder you are no longer here—so depressing. Now when I look at the pretty pink roses I see your beautiful smiling face in my mind's eye and think of our love for each other.

Rejoice with the Angels, sweetheart,

Momma

May 2018

Every day for the rest of my life I will think about Terri . . . her memories will bring laughter and tears. She will always be a part of my life. I will forever be grateful to God for choosing me to be her mother.

Prayer has made it possible for me to survive the death of my daughter. My daily prayer is for God to send his Holy Spirit to give me comfort and peace. Quoting the footprints in the sand prayer, "When you saw one set of footprints, it was then that I carried you." Yes, God has carried me every step of the way since her death. I could not possibly survive without His love. I will continue to depend on His promise, *"And the Lord, He is the One who goes before you. He will be with you. He will not leave you nor forsake you; do not fear nor be dismayed."* Deuteronomy 31:8.

I hope my experience with grief will give you understanding and direction as you travel your path. I pray God will grant you comfort and peace.

DISCLAIMER

I have tried to recreate events and conversations from my memories of them. In some instances I have changed the names of individuals and places to protect the privacy of the people involved.

ACKNOWLEDGMENTS

Kimberlyn Blum-Hyclak, author of a book of poems In The Garden of Life and Death, has been my cheerleader from the first day we met. Not only has she been the perfect editor, she has encouraged me to stay the course until the finish line. This book would not have been possible without her guidance and support. I am eternally grateful.

Glenda Manus, author of The Southern Grace Series, graciously agreed to help me publish my book on Amazon. When I called her she said she remembered well the first book she published. She needed help and now it was time for her to pay it forward.

Susan Bullard, my grief counselor, suggested I write about my life since Terri's death. It has been therapeutic for me. Many tears were shed as I wrote this book.

Ann Varnadore Beard, my cousin, who has spent 30+ years as a nonprofit administrator, championing charitable causes on both the east and west coasts, volunteered to serve as my Marketing and Public Relations Advisor. She is so excited about the book. Her excitement is infectious.

Diane Williams, my sister, came home and together we spent

hours replacing redundant words and tying up loose ends. As sisters do, we didn't always agree, but we enjoyed working together and reliving precious memories. This book has been four years in the making and Diane believed in it from day one.

God has truly blessed me with these beautiful ladies.

ABOUT THE AUTHOR

Janice Steele is Terri's mother. She is a former insurance agent and former adjunct instructor for York Technical College. She currently works as an Administrative Office Assistant with Blackmon Insurance Group. She is the founder of A New Road, a support group for parents who have lost a child, https://www. hopeforgrievingparents.com. A South Carolina native she resides in a rural area of the state with her husband. This is her first book. She can be reached through email at remember-ingterri16@gmail.com.

Made in the USA
Monee, IL
21 January 2020